HARDPRESS.NET
HOME OF HARD-TO-FIND BOOKS

Communion Services, According to the Presbyterian Form Explanations and Discourses.

by Rev. John A. Wallace

Address:
HardPress
8345 NW 66TH ST #2561
MIAMI FL 33166-2626
USA
Email: info@hardpress.net

Communion Services

REV. J. A. WALLACE

COMMUNION SERVICES

ACCORDING TO

THE PRESBYTERIAN FORM.

COMMUNION SERVICES

ACCORDING TO

THE PRESBYTERIAN FORM

BY

THE REV. J. A. WALLACE,

AUTHOR OF "PASTORAL RECOLLECTIONS," "THE PASTOR'S LEGACY,"
"ATTITUDES AND ASPECTS OF THE DIVINE REDEEMER," ETC.

"This do in remembrance of Me."—LUKE xxii. 19.

EDINBURGH:
JOHNSTONE, HUNTER, & CO.
LONDON : HAMILTON, ADAMS, & CO.

MDCCCLXV.

CONTENTS.

vi   *Contents.*

COMMUNION SERVICES.

A

INTRODUCTORY ADDRESS TO INTENDING COMMUNICANTS.

THERE were several remarkable occasions on which Christ condescended to make Himself known, after He had risen from the dead, and these, in connection with the ordinance of the Supper, are deserving of solemn and deliberate consideration.

First of all, there were two of the disciples who were journeying to a little village called Emmaus, in the neighbourhood of Jerusalem; and this being the day when Christ had risen from the dead, they were conversing together with great earnestness upon the tidings which had reached them. But, at the same time, they were very sad; for, though they were satisfied that Christ was no longer in the sepulchre, they could not believe what had been reported to them, that He was actually alive. Meantime they were joined, apparently, by a stranger, who, seemingly arrested by their great earnestness, took part in the conversation, and put the question to them, " What manner of communications are these that ye have one to another, as ye walk, and are sad ? And the one of them, whose name was Cleophas, answering said unto him, Art thou only a stranger in Jerusalem, and hast not known the things which are come to pass there in these days? And he said unto them, What things ? And they said unto him, Concerning Jesus of Nazareth, which was a prophet mighty in deed and word before God and all the people : and how the chief priests and our rulers delivered him to be condemned to death, and have crucified him. But we trusted that it had been he which should have redeemed Israel: and besides all this, to-day is the third day since these things were done. Yea, and certain women also of our company made us astonished, which were early at the sepulchre ; and when they found not his body, they came, saying, that they had also seen a vision of angels, which said that he was alive. And certain of them which were with us went to the sepulchre, and found it even so as the women had said : but him they saw not. Then he said unto them, O fools, and slow of heart to believe all that the prophets have spoken ; ought not Christ to have suffered these things, and to enter into his glory ? And beginning at Moses and

all the prophets, he expounded unto them in all
the scriptures the things concerning himself."
But their eyes were so holden that they did not
know Him. Nevertheless, when they drew nigh
unto the village whither they were going, and
when He made as if He would have gone further,
they constrained Him to abide with them, for it
was now evening, and the day was far spent.
Accordingly, He went in and tarried with them.
And it came to pass, that as He sat at meat, He
took bread, and blessed it, and brake it, and gave
it unto them. And what followed? It was
while He was in the act of communing with them
over the symbols of His broken body that their
eyes were opened, and they knew Him, and they
said one to another, as if a new light had broken
in upon them, and dispelled all the doubts and
uncertainties in which they had been involved,
"Did not our heart burn within us, while he
talked with us by the way, and while he opened
to us the scriptures?" Here, then, you have an
important fact. It was not so much by means
of the Saviour's expositions by the wayside,
though by these their hearts had been warmed,
but rather by the breaking of bread with them
at the table, that He made Himself known unto
them.

Then, again, where was it that the disciples
were, or what were they doing, when He stood

in the midst of them, and breathed upon them, and said unto them, "Receive ye the Holy Ghost?" It was not when they were separated from the company of one another, or seeking each of them for himself to commune with Him amid the solitude of his own closet; but it was when they were assembled together for social worship, and probably for the purpose of communion; it was, then, when they were together, and when the doors were shut, that He appeared suddenly in the midst of them, and said unto them, "Peace be unto you." And when He had so said, He shewed them his hands and his side; and, it is emphatically added, "Then were the disciples glad when they saw the Lord."

At that interview, however, Thomas, one of the disciples, was not present. Where he was, or what he was doing, we do not know. The sacred narrative does not furnish us with any distinct information on the subject. It might have been some work of necessity or mercy in which he was engaged. But it was not well for him to be away —to be away on so solemn an occasion—away upon the Sabbath on which Christ had risen from the dead. It had been better for him to be there; for in that case his also had been the privilege which the other disciples had enjoyed of meeting with the Saviour face to face, and sharing in the benediction of peace which He had pronounced, and experiencing the power, the enlargement, and the elevation of spirit, when He breathed upon them, and filled them with the Holy Ghost. These were privileges which the absent disciple missed, and the effect on the frame of his own spirit was so detrimental, that when the other disciples told him that they had seen the Lord, he would not credit the word which they spake to him. He gave expression only to the feelings of a peevish, disappointed, and unbelieving mind, saying unto them, " Except I shall see in his hands the print of the nails, and put my finger into the print of the nails, and thrust my hand into his side, I will not believe."

But after eight days, on the return of the Sabbath, or on the first day of the week, the disciples were again assembled together, and the absent and unbelieving disciple was now in the midst of them, and, apparently for his sake, the remarkable interview was repeated ; for when they were together, and when the doors were shut, Jesus appeared again in the midst of them, and said unto them, " Peace be unto you." Then turning to Thomas, He saith unto him, " Reach hither thy finger, and behold my hands; and reach hither thy hand, and thrust it into my side: and be not faithless but believing. And Thomas answered and said unto him," as if all his doubts had dissolved and disappeared, " My Lord, and my God."

And then, still farther, in regard to the third time that Jesus shewed Himself to the disciples after He had risen from the dead, what were the circumstances, or how were they employed ? It was not amid the watches of the night, when they had cast their nets into the Sea of Tiberias, and had caught nothing ; nor amid the light of the morning, when Jesus stood upon the shore, for at that time they did not know Him ; but when He directed them to cast the net upon the right side of the ship, and when straightway it was filled with a great multitude of fishes ; then the light began to break in upon them, for the beloved disciple whispered to Peter, " It is the Lord." And then, when they were come to land, and He sat down with them, and took bread, and divided it amongst them, we are led to understand that none of the disciples, not even the most incredulous, durst, or needed to ask Him, " Who art thou ? knowing that it was the Lord."

These interesting incidents emphatically indicate that Christ is specially to be known in the breaking of bread, or at the communion table. He may meet with you elsewhere ; for He is not strictly confined to temples, or places made with hands. He is near unto all that call upon

Him. And if your desires are towards Him, and towards the remembrance of His name, He may meet with you amid the solitude of your closets, in your journeyings by the wayside, amid the turmoil of your business concerns, at the cross, at the mercy-seat, at the open fountain, at the wells of salvation, on the bed of sickness, amid the shadows of death. But if there be any place under the canopy of heaven where you are warranted to come with the weight of your heaviest burdens, or the urgency of your largest and most aspiring desires—any place under the canopy of heaven where the Saviour is most likely to meet with you, and to give to you the most transcendent manifestations of His glory, it is at the table of communion which He Himself has spread, and which is not only covered with the emblems of His broken body and shed blood, but where, when the disciples are together, and the doors are shut, He Himself is sitting.

The ordinance, when viewed merely in its outward aspect, is exceedingly simple. The description of it is comprised in a few words, and these so plain, that a little child might be able to understand them. But, simple as it is, it opens to the eye of faith a field of vision the most comprehensive and the most glorious which it is possible for the human mind to conceive.

B

On the one hand, you behold the Saviour amid all the accompaniments of mortal sorrow, encompassed with an infidel multitude, transfixed to the accursed tree, with the pale ensigns of death on His countenance, the solid earth rending beneath the awful spectacle, and the radiant heavens all clothed with the garments of mourning. On the other hand, you behold Him amid all the accompaniments of celestial glory, attended with a retinue of ten thousand times ten thousand and thousands of thousands, seated amid the effulgence of the everlasting throne, with the lustre of many crowns beaming from His forehead, and the entire universe standing in awe of His great and terrible majesty. To the one, you are invited to go back, that your hearts may be softened with the sight of the Saviour's sorrow—that, looking upon Him whom you have pierced, you may mourn and be in bitterness, even as one mourneth for an only child. To the other, you are invited to look forward, that your hearts may be cheered with the anticipation of the Saviour's glory—that, looking out for the day when He shall come in the clouds of heaven, and all His holy angels with Him, you may lift up your heads, because the day of your redemption draweth nigh, and may be filled with joys that are unspeakable and full of glory. Here it sets before you pre-

sent mercies, light amid your darkness, comfort
in your afflictions, strength in the midst of your
weakness, consolation amid the bitterness of
your trials. For it invites you to shew forth
Christ's death, the foundation of every hope, the
source of every comfort, the germ of every promise, the theme of every song of praise. And it
reserves for you hereafter the final destruction
of all your enemies, the resurrection of your
bodies from the grave, the acceptance of your
persons at the bar of judgment, your admission
through the gates into the celestial city, your
actual and everlasting investiture with all the
rights and immunities of heaven. For it invites
you to look forward to Christ's coming again,
carrying your faith over and beyond the solemn
changes that await yourselves, or the terrible
commotions that may take place upon the earth,
ere the time of the end shall be, and, instead of
leaving you to sink amid the heaving billows,
or to lose the anchor of your faith amid the
gathering storm, setting before you a haven of
rest to which the troubled spirit may look forward and be at peace. For Christ shall come
again ; and, having that event to rest upon, you
may safely leave the issue of all events, however
dark, in the hand of God, believing that the
coming of the Son of man shall clear up all
mysteries, and put a period to the triumphing

of the wicked, and fix the stamp of everlasting
perfection on the redemption of all the saints.

In this way the ordinance carries you back,
not only to the great eternity that is past, but
forward to the great eternity that is yet to come;
while it brings before you, either in experience
or in prospect, all spiritual blessings in heavenly
places through Christ Jesus, that so, according
to the utmost measure of your capacities, you
may be filled with all the fulness of God.

And then, still farther, it brings you into close
and vital fellowship with all the saints, whether
they be on earth, or whether they be in heaven.
Christ's heart has room enough for the whole
household, from the fathers of ancient days to
the least of the little ones that inherit the kingdom of heaven. If, therefore, you get near to
the Master's heart, and have fellowship with
Him, you may have fellowship at the same time
with the whole family of the redeemed, with the
old ancestry of the patriarchs and prophets, with
the glorious company of the apostles, with the
noble army of the martyrs, with every name
that is renowned amongst the saints that are
below, with every name that is written in the
book of life that is above.

The tables that are spread here are but small.
The eye can take them in at a single glance.
You can easily reckon up the numbers that sit

down at them. They are quickly filled, and they
are soon emptied again. But there is much
which is not seen with the eye of sense which
may be seen with the eye of faith. That eye,
when the light is shining, and the scales are
cleared away, can carry you into a region where
the tables have no visible termination, and the
feast of communion is spread for a multitude
which no man can number. The lower seats
may be occupied by the members of the Church
that is still militant, weeping, suffering, tempted,
helpless, needy, dying saints. It is these only,
and but a small detachment of them, that are
perceptible to the eye of sense. But, far beyond
the range of the visible, there is a vast territory
which nothing but the eye of faith can see,
covered with ranges of seats, in numbers that are
infinite, constructed like unto the similitude of
thrones, rising tier beyond tier, and terminating, if they can be said to terminate at all, in
the upper and the far off galleries of the great
eternity; and these are occupied by the members of the Church triumphant, by the regnant
and the glorified, whose days of mourning have
been brought to an everlasting close. It may be
a voice of weeping and of supplication that is
rising from the lower platform, a voice of triumph
and of melody that is bursting from golden
harps, and from glad voices, from the upper

circles that are crowded with the high ranks and
orders of the redeemed; but Christ, the Master
of the feast, is in the midst of them both, and
His eye is fixed on the one as well as on the
other. The tears of the mourner are as precious
to Him as the crowns of the glorified. His ear
is as attentive to the cries and groanings of the
downcast and the disconsolate, as it is to the
songs and adorations of heaven's bright and glorified hosts. He has something in common with
them both; for He was once a suffering, and
He is now a glorified Redeemer. And they also
have something in common with Him; for some
of them are still mourners, passing through
great tribulation, and others of them are now
ransomed from their troubles, and all tears have
been wiped from their eyes. And then, moreover, they have something in common with one
another—the Church triumphant with the Church
militant, and the Church militant with the Church
triumphant; for the one is what the other once
was, cast down and oppressed with the heaviness
of grief, yet looking up from the depths, and
waiting to be lifted to the same glory to which
the other has risen. The hand which wipes the
tears from the eyes of the mourner is the same
that puts the jewelled crown on the heads of the
glorified. That hand is Christ's, and the table
at which He presides, and the temple which He

fills with His glory, has its ascending stairs, and its channels of communication with the great marriage supper that is above. In both cases the Master of the feast is the same, and, though the guests may wear a different aspect, yet they all belong to the same family, and the fellowship of the one is identical with the fellowship of the other. They are clothed in the same righteousness. They glory in the same cross. They cling to the same Father. They claim the same heritage and the same heaven. Whether they be sitting at the table above, or at the table below, they have but one Head. That Head is Christ, and they all are children to Him, and brethren to one another.

Therefore, dear friends, when you come to the table of communion it behoves you to come both in faith and in love—in faith towards Christ, and in love one toward another. You cannot have fellowship with the Master, and stand aloof from the members of His family; and the same impediments which may hinder you from communing with a brother who may be sitting close beside you at the table, cannot fail to close the door of hope in the Valley of Achor, and to shut you out from all comfortable converse, both with the loving Redeemer and with all belonging to Him, who are walking amid the rich vineyards of Engedi.

But if all walls of partition are broken down, and the graces of the Spirit are brought into lively exercise, there cannot be a doubt that the Saviour will make Himself known to you at the table, giving you such glimpses of His own glory as will not only absorb the bitterness of your most poignant griefs, but carry you through a great wide door opened in heaven, to refresh your wearied spirits with the fellowship of the glorified amid the splendours and the felicities of heaven.

MEDITATIONS FOR THE CLOSET.

I.—EVERLASTING LOVE.

"I HAVE loved thee with an everlasting love: therefore with lovingkindness have I drawn thee."—JER. xxxi. 3. In the prospect of sitting down at the communion table, let me meditate on this most marvellous declaration of the Saviour's love; and may my heart be touched with a live coal from off the altar of God, that so every unholy feeling may be utterly consumed within me, and nothing left but the glowing gratitude which the love of Christ kindles, and which, when once kindled, abides always, and lives for ever.

"I have loved thee." Is it really so, O my Saviour? Hast Thou indeed loved *me*—not an angel, nor an archangel, nor a seraph, nor a saint in glory, but an outcast from the favour and fellowship of God, a wanderer from the

c

paths of righteousness and peace, a rebel against the righteous government of Heaven, a being not only unnecessary to Thy existence, and undeserving of Thy compassions, but a blot amid the glories of Thy kingdom, and a curse to the moral and intelligent universe of God !

But hast *Thou* loved me, even Thou—not a being as helpless, as polluted, as miserable, as degraded as myself, but the brightness of the Father's glory, and the express image of His person, who fillest eternity and immensity with Thy presence, who dwellest within the high and holy place, and whose blessedness is for ever independent of the purest and the loftiest of created beings !

Yea, hast Thou loved me, not with the cold, the distant, the languid affection that wavers in the breasts of capricious, fallible, dying men, but with the strength and purity of a love which no affliction could extinguish, and no agonies of death could destroy—a love which brought Thee down from the mansions of celestial glory, and constrained Thee to clothe Thyself with the infirmities of my own frail nature, that every doubt and suspicion might be dispelled within me, by beholding the marvellous manifestations of Thy regard, and gazing on the bitter tears which Thou hast shed, and marking the mortal agonies Thou hast felt, and thrusting my hand into the print of the nails that have torn and lacerated Thy blessed feet !

Hast Thou loved me, moreover, not with the sensibility of a transient emotion—an emotion that glows brightly for a while, and then expires for ever—but loved me with an *everlasting* love, —loved me before the songs of the morning stars were sung, or the glories of creation were scattered through the vacancies of space,—loved me through all the dispensations of Thy providence and grace from the earliest of times,—loved me amid the solemn mysteries of Calvary, when nailed by bloody hands to the accursed tree,— loved me through all the scenes of suffering and of change through which I myself have been led, till brought to the mercies of this wondrous hour !

And since Thou hast loved me from the days of eternity, wilt Thou still continue to love me with a love that is everlasting still ? Is there nothing in heaven, or in earth, or in hell, that can blot me from the book of Thy remembrance, or drive me beyond the boundaries of Thy love ? Wilt Thou think of me amid all the vicissitudes through which I am destined to pass, ere this mortal pilgrimage shall be brought to a close ? Wilt Thou strengthen me for every duty ? Wilt Thou guide me through every difficulty ? Wilt Thou sustain me under every trial ? Wilt

Thou pillow my head on Thy bosom amid the
deep and overwhelming waters of death; and,
amid a vast, boundless, and interminable eternity, wilt Thou love me with a love that is everlasting still?   Oh! marvellous condescension,
awful mystery of godliness, compassions without beginning, love beyond expression, and love
without end!

But art thou sure, O my soul, that the
blessed Saviour hath cherished the love that is
everlasting even for thee?   Look into the inmost recesses of thine own heart; mark the
hole of the pit out of which thou hast been
drawn; trace the windings of the path by
which thou hast been led, and say if it be with
lovingkindness that He hath drawn thee?   Hath
He drawn thee by the lovingkindness of His
invitations—drawn thee by the lovingkindness
of His promises—drawn thee by the lovingkindness of His warnings—drawn thee by the lovingkindness of His judgments—drawn thee from
the vanities of the world, from the company of
the ungodly, from the snares of the devil, from
the rebellion and the abominations of an evil
heart of unbelief—drawn thee by His word, by
His providence, by His ministers, by His ordinances, by His Spirit—till He hath constrained
thee to seek, and enabled thee to find, the sure
and everlasting portion of thy soul in Himself?

If so be that He hath drawn thee with lovingkindness, therefore hath He loved thee even
with an everlasting love.

II.—THE EARNEST INQUIRY.

" Tell me, O thou whom my soul loveth,
where thou feedest, where thou makest thy
flock to rest at noon : for why should I be as
one that turneth aside by the flocks of thy companions ?"—CANT. i. 7.

" The flocks of thy companions." I have
often mingled with the flocks of Thy companions,
but it is not the flocks of Thy companions that
can satisfy my soul. Yea, in times past I have
come to the ordinances of Thy grace, to the
green pastures and the still waters where the
flocks of Thy companions feed. But how comfortless are all the ordinances of Thy grace without Thee ! It is Thou, O Thou whom my
soul seeketh ; it is Thou, O Thou whom my soul
loveth. Tell me where Thou feedest, where
Thou makest Thy flock to rest at noon.

Thy secret is with them that fear Thee, and
Thou revealest Thyself unto Thine own. But
wilt Thou indeed reveal Thyself unto me ? Alas !

what claims have I on Thy love and Thy tender
mercies? What claims have I, a lost sheep, a
wanderer from Thy fold, an alien from the flocks
of Thy companions, a rebel against the principles
of Thy holy law, a neglecter of the riches of
Thy free and sovereign grace? What claims
have I? I have no claims, unless they are to be
found in guilt, and waywardness, and rebellion,
and misery.

What hast Thou done unto me? Thou hast
thought of me, and watched over me, and guid-
ed me, and dealt very patiently with me, and
offered to heal me, and to help me, and to feed
me, and to shelter me, and to be the shadow of
a great rock to me, and to be my refuge, and
my righteousness, and my strength, and my
confidence, and my glory, and my all in all.
But what have I done unto Thee, O Thou
tenderest of shepherds? I have forgotten Thee.
I have forsaken Thee. I have rebelled against
Thee. Yet I have not done it without warnings the most solemn, the most awakening.
Even at the time when I was mad upon my
idols, and rushing recklessly into the vanities
and pollutions of the world, I heard Thy voice
behind me, crying with the most beseeching
earnestness, " Turn ye, turn ye from your evil
ways, for why will ye die?" Yea, crying with
a voice so full of tenderness that it smote upon

my heart, and almost arrested me. For it seemed to be saying, Thou art wounding thy Shepherd as with the wound of an enemy. Nevertheless, I stopped not. I stifled the rising conviction. I fled from the voice of my Shepherd, till that voice was drowned amid vanity and lies. But I have met with a righteous recompense. My rebellion hath been my ruin and my misery, and my soul is desolate within me. Yet it is the thought of Thy tenderness that wounds me. It is the recollection of Thy deep compassions that afflicts me with pangs of agony that I cannot bear. It is the sounding of Thy bowels and mercies that turns my strength into corruption, and my voice into the voice of one that weeps. " Behold, O Lord: for I am in distress, my bowels are troubled, mine heart is turned within me, for I have grievously rebelled." " Have mercy upon me, O God, according to thy lovingkindness: according unto the multitude of thy tender mercies blot out my transgressions. Wash me throughly from mine iniquity, and cleanse me from my sin. For I acknowledge my transgressions: and my sin is ever before me. Against thee, thee only, have I sinned, and done this evil in thy sight." Therefore doth my heart cry unto Thee from the lowest depths, " Tell me, O thou whom my soul seeketh, O thou whom my soul loveth,

where thou feedest, where thou makest thy flock
to rest at noon : for why should I be as one that
turneth aside by the flocks of thy companions ?"

III.—THE VOICE OF CONSOLATION.

" Comfort ye, comfort ye my people, saith
your God. Speak ye comfortably to Jerusalem,
and cry unto her, that her warfare is accomplished, that her iniquity is pardoned : for she
hath received of the Lord's hand double for all
her sins."—Isa. xl. 1, 2. Whose words are these,
O my soul, so rich, so precious, so full of
power, so full of tenderness, falling with the
freshness of their consolations on the downcast
and the broken-hearted ? They are not the
words of some created being, as needy, as undeserving, as comfortless as thyself. They are
the words of God, even of that God whose heart
is an ocean of tenderness, from whose throne
issueth the fountain of living waters, whose
hand wipeth away all tears from the eyes of His
saints, and who openeth even in the wilderness
wells of consolation wherewith to refresh the
souls of the weary, the desponding, and the
broken-hearted. It is the voice of the very

Being whose power summoned all worlds into existence, and who upholds them—whose eye searches all spirits and discerns them—His voice that saith, "Comfort ye, comfort ye my people."

"My people!" Not the wicked, nor the profane, nor the Sabbath-breaker, nor the unthankful, nor the intemperate, nor the impenitent, nor the unbelieving. For them there is warning, and instruction, and correction; but for them there is no consolation; and for the consolation which God confers they themselves have no relish, no desire. But "comfort ye, comfort ye my people"—the penitent, the believing, the humble-minded, the contrite ones. Comfort ye them, for they are far away from their home. They are wandering through the bleakness of the wilderness. They are passing through the land of their enemies. Comfort ye them, lest they be discouraged with the greatness of their difficulties, or oppressed with the weight of their burdens, or appalled by the darkness of their prospects. Comfort ye them, for they are My people, the sheep of My own fold, the object of My everlasting compassions, the travail of the Redeemer's soul in its agony, the heirs of the purchased and promised inheritance, the people whose souls' desires are towards Me and towards the remembrance of My name.

D

But wherefore, O my soul, is this consolation sent unto thee? On thy part has there been no forgetfulness of His mercies, no discontentment with His providence, no striving with His Holy Spirit, no misimprovement of distinguished privileges, no violation of sacred engagements, no neglecting of incumbent duties, no pride, no self-righteousness, no rebellion, and yet hast thou not received at the Lord's hand double for all thy sins? Double for all thy sins! Strange language that. What can be the meaning of it? Is it double vengeance, double punishment, double condemnation? That, beyond all question, I had reason to expect, and had my recompense come to me from any other hand but the hand of God, that I might have received. But God's ways are not like unto my ways; God's thoughts are not like unto my thoughts. For though I have made Him to serve with my sins, and wearied Him with mine iniquities, yet from His hands have I received a recompense, a double recompense, a recompense of good in the place of a recompense of evil. He hath doubled His patience, that He might gain the victory over my aggravated and outrageous rebellion. He hath doubled His watchfulness, that He might never lose sight of me amid the waywardness of my wanderings. He hath doubled His mercy till it hath swollen up from a great deep, and risen to the very heavens, and come over and covered the whole mountain of mine iniquities. Thus have I received of the Lord's hand double for all my sins. But why? Just because my warfare hath been accomplished, just because my sin hath been pardoned—my sin hath been atoned for. If my sin had not been atoned for, and atoned for by the blood of the Lamb that was slain, most assuredly my sin must have been punished, and punished in myself. If my warfare had not been accomplished, and accomplished through the power of Him who is mighty to save, most assuredly the victory had been lost, and my perdition had been achieved. But because, through the righteousness and merit of the great Mediator, my warfare hath been accomplished, and my iniquity hath been pardoned, therefore have I received double for all my sins, whilst unto me, clinging to the cross, and resting on the Saviour's finished work, is the voice of this consolation sent, " Comfort ye, comfort ye my people, saith your God. Speak ye comfortably to Jerusalem, and cry unto her, that her warfare is accomplished, that her iniquity is pardoned: for she hath received of the Lord's hand double for all her sins."

IV.—THE PERSONAL CALL.

" Fear not: for I have redeemed thee, I have called thee by thy name; thou art mine."—Hast Thou really called me, even me, not only a creature, a feeble creature, a creature whose foundation is in the dust, and who is crushed before the moth, but a sinful creature, a creature laden with iniquity, a creature covered with the most loathsome pollutions, a creature sunk into the lowest depths of moral corruption, a sinner charged with the most heinous of all wickedness, with the most atrocious of all guilt—the guilt of crucifying the Son of God afresh, and putting Him to an open shame!

And hast Thou called me by my name, a name which is registered in the Book of Life, and inscribed on the palms of Thy hands, and set amid the rich garnishing of most precious stones on the golden girdle which Thou wearest amid the splendours of the celestial temple, and when conducting the services of the golden altar that is before the throne—called me, not by a general or indiscriminate call ; a call as applicable to other men as to myself, but called me by a special and peculiar call; a call in regard to which there can be no misapprehension and no mistake ; a call which has fallen upon my ear, and entered into the innermost recesses of my heart; a call as clear, as distinct, as intelligible, as irresistible, as if Thou hadst appeared before me, and singled me out from amid the masses of a dense multitude, and said to me with an audible voice, and by the utterance of my own name, "Thou art mine"!

But when didst Thou call me? Ah, not when I was calling upon Thee, calling loudly, calling with all my heart. Hadst Thou waited till I had first called upon Thee, I never had been called at all. I had still continued wandering upon the mountains of vanity, drawing water out of broken cisterns, enclosing myself in refuges of lies, and at last perishing in the midst of my own corruptions. But Thou hast followed me even into the wilderness, and laid Thy strong hand upon me, and arrested me by the sounding of Thy bowels and of Thy mercies. And if the call has taken effect, and my soul has been made willing in the day of Thy power, the inference is irresistible, that from first to last it has been a call of grace—free, sovereign, unmerited grace—and therefore the full and undivided glory does rightly and everlastingly belong, not unto myself, for in myself there dwelleth no good thing, but unto Him who hath loved me and called me, and given Himself for me. " Bless the Lord, O my

soul: and all that is within me, bless his holy
name. Bless the Lord, O my soul, and forget
not all his benefits: who forgiveth all thine iniquities; who healeth all thy diseases; who re-
deemeth thy life from destruction; who crowneth
thee with lovingkindness and tender mercies."
"What shall I render unto the Lord for all his
benefits toward me? I will take the cup of salvation, and call upon the name of the Lord. I
will pay my vows unto the Lord now in the presence of all his people. In the courts of the
Lord's house, in the midst of thee, O Jerusalem.
Praise ye the Lord."

V.—THE BELIEVER'S SURETY.

"And one shall say unto him, What are these
wounds in thine hands"?—How comes it to pass
that one so holy is yet suffering so intensely?
—that one so highly exalted is yet plunged into
the depths of the lowest humiliation? "What
are these wounds in thine hands," or in Thy feet,
or in Thy pierced side, or in Thy bleeding brow?
What is the answer which the sufferer Himself
returns? The answer is this. They are "those
with which I was wounded in the house," or,

perhaps, as it may be more significantly expressed, in the *place* " of my friends." Is that the real position which Christ occupies? Does He actually hold the character of His people's Surety? Has He been wounded for their transgressions? Has He been bruised for their iniquities? Has the chastisement of their peace been laid upon Him? And is it by His stripes that they are healed? It is not, therefore, enough that I look upon my own sins as deserving of the wrath and curse of God, but I must contemplate them, if I rely upon Christ as my Saviour, as being laid on the head of the Surety, and subjecting Him to the very punishment which I myself had incurred, and which but for Him must have been inflicted upon myself; and I must think of that punishment as being inflicted by God, for there is another party involved in the solemn transaction. Christ is not dealing exclusively with me, nor am I dealing exclusively with Christ. My iniquities are the ostensible occasion of the Redeemer's suffering, yet the suffering is not inflicted directly by myself, but at the hands of eternal Justice, whose flaming sword is drawn from its scabbard, and plunged by the Lord of hosts into the bosom of the very Being who was His own fellow, the brightness of His glory, the express image of His person, in whom His very soul delighted. And what is the result? The wounds

that were inflicted on Him in the room of His
friends, can never more be inflicted on them,
for He has exhausted the penalty. Justice is
completely satisfied. The sword hath returned
again to its scabbard. And if I have really accepted Him as my Surety, and have taken my
stand upon the ground of His finished and
attested work, there is no power in the universe
that can subject me to the condemnation of a
broken law, or invalidate my right to the blessings which He hath purchased with His blood.

But let me be careful to maintain my true
position, to act up to my high privileges, and to
keep within my own province. Let me make
free use, at all times and in all circumstances, of
the benefit of Christ's finished work, but let me
never take upon myself the burden of my own
guilt. That were to trench upon the prerogatives of my Surety, and to resume, illegally, and
in violation of my covenant engagement, what I
have already devolved upon Christ, and what
Christ has not refused to appropriate. Even
the sins that were committed by myself are
no longer my own. They are Christ's. And
what hath He done with them? He hath nailed
them to the accursed tree, that, though red as
crimson, the blood of the great atonement might
make them white as snow; or He hath buried
them in the grave of an everlasting forgetfulness,

that so their festering corruptions might not
only be removed out of my sight, but that their
voices, though loud as the thunders of Sinai,
might be silent as the tongue of the dead man
that is reposing in the sepulchre; or He hath
taken them up by the grasp of His almightiness,
and, like the millstone of the great archangel,
He hath hurled them down into the profoundest
abysses of the unfathomable ocean, that so,
though great in number as the sands that lie
scattered on the sea-shore, they should pass en-
tirely out of sight, and come up in memorial
against me no more for ever. Beware, then, O
my soul, of withdrawing your sins from the cross,
where Christ Himself has nailed them, or drag-
ging them from the grave in which Christ Himself has buried them, or fetching them up from
the abysses into which Christ has cast them.
For, in that case, the iron nails which you have
loosened from their hold upon the cross will
pass like a burning ploughshare through the
flesh of thine own heart, and the festering corruption which the grave had covered will spread
like a noisome pestilence through all the
chambers of thy soul, and the sins which are
more in number than the sands of the sea-shore
will go over your head like a burden which you
can never bear—a burden sufficient to sink you
into the lowest hell. Leave your sins, O my

B

soul, in Christ's hands, and where Christ has
placed them. Without your help He can dispose
of them to the perfect satisfaction of eternal
justice. Resting upon your own shoulders they
will prove a perpetual torment to you, darkening
all your prospects, and pouring wormwood into
the cup of your sweetest consolations; but in
Christ's hands you need not be afraid of them;
they can never hurt you.

VI.—VINEYARDS IN THE WILDERNESS.

" Behold, I will allure her, and bring her into
the wilderness, and speak comfortably unto her,
and I will give her her vineyards from thence,
and the valley of Achor for a door of hope, and
she shall sing there as in the days of her youth."
—Remember, O my soul, that God has various
places of meeting with His people, and making
Himself known to them, but they have not
always, to the outward eye, an aspect of great
pleasantness. Sometimes, indeed, He may bring
you into the banqueting house, in the very
palace of the King, where He spreads out before
you a feast of fat things, and where His banner
over you being love, you sit down under His

shadow with great delight, and His fruit is sweet to your taste. Sometimes He may walk with you in the vineyards of Engedi, where the rose of Sharon and the lily of the valley are blooming, and the whole atmosphere is perfumed with myrrh and frankincense, and saffron and cinnamon. Sometimes He may lead you through the secret places of the stairs, and take you up into the King's gallery, and permit you to look forth from the open lattice, greatly enlarging your prospects, and giving you the first-fruits of the land that is afar off. But there are other places where the sound of His voice is not unfrequently to be heard,—pits, dark and deep, out of which no other hand but His own can draw you—furnaces, glowing with living fire, where no other form but that of the Son of man can temper the heat, and purge away the dross—valleys of thick darkness and of awful solitude, where nothing but His own rod can guide, His own staff support, His own presence cheer—great wildernesses covered with the stones of emptiness, and darkened with the shadows of death, where nothing but His own voice can scatter the gloom, and bring down help and deliverance from heaven. " Behold, I will allure thee, and bring thee into the wilderness." The wilderness ! It is not an attractive word. It grates harshly on the ear. It awakens no gladsome feeling in the heart. But let me never forget that many wonderful sights have been seen in the wilderness,—bushes burning with devouring fire, and not a leaf of them consumed; rocks, harder than adamant, yielding rivers of living water by a single touch; serpents of brass set up in the view of a great camp, and imparting life to men dying of mortal wounds by a single look; tables spread in the midst of bleakness and desolation, that are all covered with angels' food; vast fields reclaimed from their sterility, and clad with vineyards loaded with the richest clusters of the grapes of Canaan.

How soothing to the soul, fainting beneath the pressure of its burdens, brought low through sore distress, and disquieted with many sorrows, to betake itself, in the dark and cloudy day, to the light and consolation of the recorded promise, "Behold, I will allure thee." This is not the rigid discipline of a taskmaster, nor the over-bearing oppression of an enemy, else the soul might be disposed to rebel. It breathes the spirit of gentleness. It addresses itself to the heart with the sweet, attractive, irresistible persuasiveness of love. What soul that knows the Saviour can stand out against the drawing of such tenderness, or hesitate for a moment to follow Him, though He is alluring into the wilderness, not only away from outward comforts, or from bodily health, or from Christian fellowship, or from active usefulness, or from public ordinances, or from the very fountains whence consolation seemed most likely to be drawn, but into the wilderness, dark, waste-howling, solitary, and into the valley of Achor, which is the valley of trouble, and of pits, and of snares, and of the shadows of death. Nevertheless, it is well to follow the Saviour even there; for, even in the wilderness He provides a place of vineyards, a place of fruitfulness, a place of spiritual abundance, a place of reviving consolations; and in the valley of trouble He also opens a door of hope—a door whose lintels are sprinkled with the blood that cleanses from the pollution of all sin, and speaketh peace amid the disquietude of all sorrow; a door of hope leading into a field of promise the most fertile, the most flourishing— a field of promise where, for the healing of all bleeding wounds, there are leaves dropping in their fragrancy from the trees of immortality, and streams, for the refreshing of all sorrowful souls, flowing from that mighty river that maketh glad the city of our God, and prospects of everlasting glory stretching afar into the better land where there is a fulness of joy, and pleasures which are at God's right hand for ever.

Happy the soul that follows the Saviour into this wilderness, however desolate, and into this valley of trouble, however trying! Thence are

the sweetest of its comforts. For it is not amid
the plenitude of other mercies, when the soul is
surfeited with rich dainties, that it draws water
with the greatest joy out of the wells of salvation. It is the faintness, almost unto death,
which the soul feels amid the solitude and sterility of the wilderness, that imparts the richest
relish to the wine of Lebanon ; while the land
of promise is invested with an air of more enchanting loveliness when viewed through the
door of hope that is opened in the valley of
Achor.

Blessed Saviour, hast Thou led me, either by
the allurements of Thy voice, or by the heavy
chastisements of Thy hand, away from the outward comforts which I prized the most, and
brought me into the wilderness and the valley
of Achor ? still to Thy holy will I desire to bow,
and Thy footsteps would I follow whithersoever
Thou leadest ; for Thou alone art the light of
my countenance, the strength of my heart, and
the portion of my soul. Oh, leave me not for a
moment, nor let Thy sweet comforts forsake me.
Even in the wilderness do Thou give me the
place of vineyards, and in the valley of trouble
do Thou open the door of hope, that, relieved
from the pressure of my burdens, and enjoying
the peace which passeth all understanding, I
may sing before Thee as in the days of my youth.

VII.—THE CLOUD BLOTTED OUT.

" I have blotted out, as a thick cloud, thy transgressions, and, as a cloud, thy sins : return unto me ; for I have redeemed thee."—Mark, O my soul, it is God that here speaks to you. To His voice you are invited to listen, His hand you are summoned to trace, His work on which you are warranted to rest, His word which you are commanded to believe. And He is not a man that He should lie, nor the son of man that He should repent. He is the same yesterday, to-day, and for ever, without any variableness or the least shadow of turning. But what are the terms which He uses ? " I have blotted out, as a thick cloud, thy transgressions, and, as a cloud, thy sins." That is the statement of God. It is not the giving of a promise which remains yet to be fulfilled, or whose fulfilment is dependent on any conditions which it rests with thee to implement. It is the statement of a fact already past, and which nothing in heaven, or on earth, or in hell, can ever cancel or annul. Take, then, this statement of God. View it in all its bearings, give to it the legitimate meaning which it bears, and make it the object of a simple and implicit faith, and this one fact

stands out palpable, and apparent, and impregnable, that the redemption is already achieved,
the ransom is already paid, the middle wall of
partition between you and God is broken down,
and the very iniquities which shut you out from
the light of His countenance, and fill you with
horror and alarm, are all blotted out and taken
away. If, therefore, there are any hindrances
remaining, these are not on the side of God.
For in that case He never could have asked, or
permitted, or commanded you to return. Nay,
He had passed sentence against you, and banished you for ever out of His sight. The hindrances are of your own making, and the clouds
that are still intervening are not generated
around the throne of God, nor are they such as
come down from the serene bosom of heaven,
where the tempests never rise, and the sun is
always shining, but such only as go up even to
the great firmament from the face of this fallen
world, and from the vile and festering corruptions of an evil heart of unbelief.

" I have blotted out, as a thick cloud, thy
transgressions, and, as a cloud, thy sins." That
is the thing which God hath done; and observe,
O my soul, what follows, " Return unto me."
If the obstacles on the side of God had not been
removed, return on your part had been impossible. You had not been warranted to return,

and you never could have done it, if you had been so inclined. But the invitation is addressed to you, " Return unto me." And why? what is the reason? The reason is this, " I have redeemed thee." The ransom is paid, the thick cloud is dispelled, the way of reconciliation is cleared from every obstruction, sprinkled with the purifying and the peace-speaking blood, and opened, without money and without price, even to the guiltiest and the chiefest of sinners. Hence the invitation, " Return unto me." And when the invitation is accepted, and the wandering and the backsliding sinner returns, there is not only joy amongst the angels of God, but the whole universe, the heavens, and the earth, and all that they contain, are invited to join their voices together in one grand chorus of adoration. " Sing, O ye heavens; for the Lord hath done it: shout, ye lower parts of the earth; break forth into singing, ye mountains, O forest, and every tree therein; for the Lord hath redeemed Jacob, and glorified himself in Israel."

VIII.—THE TABERNACLES OF GOD.

" O send out thy light and thy truth: let them lead me; let them bring me unto thy holy

hill, and to thy tabernacles. Then will I go
unto the altar of God, unto God my exceeding
joy: yea, upon the harp will I praise thee, O
God my God. Why art thou cast down, O my
soul? and why art thou disquieted within me?
hope in God: for I shall yet praise him, who is
the health of my countenance, and my God."—
These, O my soul, were the aspirations of the
sweet singer of Israel, at a time when the waves
and billows of the heaviest affliction were going
over him, and the darkest clouds were overshadowing the brightest of his hopes. Yet it
was not the pressure of any outward calamity
that weighed most heavily on his spirit, or which
brought him down to the depths of the lowest
distress. The severity of personal affliction, the
oppression and the triumph of mortal enemies,
were to him as nothing when compared with
the sadness and desolation of spirit which he
experienced when shut out from the tabernacles
and the altar of God. It was the recollection
of these precious privileges, when he had gone
up to the house of God with the voice of joy
and praise, along with the multitude that kept
holyday, that came back to his soul with such
overwhelming power, constraining him to cry
out, in the agony and earnestness of his spirit,
" As the hart panteth after the water brooks,
so panteth my soul after thee, O God. My soul

thirsteth for God, for the living God : when shall I come and appear before God ? "

The privilege denied to the Psalmist is one that is vouchsafed unto you, O my soul. But unless you have somewhat of the same deep experience, the same fervent love, the same earnest desire, it is not to be expected that the ordinance, however precious in itself, will be unto thee the source of any refreshment, the fountain of any consolation, or the occasion of any spiritual joy. Well, therefore, does it become thee to join in the importunate prayer, " O send out thy light and thy truth"—not, indeed, for the mere purpose of bringing thee to the ordinances from which others may be excluded, but for the purpose of bringing thee with right affections, with enlarged desires, with earnest expectations, having thy soul and all that is within thee going out fervently towards Christ, and towards the remembrance of His name. Without these thou mayest go to the altar of God, but there will be no living sacrifice; and to His tabernacles, but to thee there will be no revelation of the glory of God in the face of Jesus Christ; and unto God's holy hill, but there will be no bright and soul-reviving prospects into the glories of the promised land. If thy soul was dark before, it will be dark still ; or dead before, it will be dead still ; or worldly before, it will be worldly still. But if the light, and the truth, and the Spirit of God are sent forth, the sanctuary will not only be filled by the Divine glory, but the provisions of Christ's table, which to the careless and the unbelieving have no meaning, will be life and spirit unto thee—His body will be meat indeed, His blood will be drink indeed.

With such a cheering prospect let this, then, be the language of thy heart, " Why art thou cast down, O my soul ? and why art thou disquieted within me ? " Why art thou cast down with the fears that live in the memory of the past, with the doubts which embitter the enjoyments of the present, with the apprehensions which darken the prospects of the future? Still trust in God. In the days that are past, thou hast often looked to His power for assistance, to His wisdom for direction, to His grace for the sweet tokens of His love. But thou canst not say that His power hath ever failed, or that His wisdom hath ever erred, that His eye hath ever ceased to regard thee with tenderness, or His ear been ever closed to the voice of thy prayers. Then, " why art thou cast down, O my soul ? and why art thou disquieted within me ? " Still hope in God, whose power thou hast already experienced, and whose love thou hast already felt. And though perplexity and distress should surround thee on every side, and the darkness which dims thy spiritual vision should prevent thee from tracing the operation of His hands, still hope in God, and glorify the perfections of His character by an unlimited dependence on His wisdom, by an unsuspecting confidence in His love. And thou shalt not hope in vain. Though distressing be thy present circumstances, though dark be thy future prospects, erelong He will appoint unto thee beauty for ashes, the oil of joy for mourning, and the garments of praise for the spirit of heaviness, and bring thee at last to that bright and blessed land, where no clouds shall ever darken around thee, and no calamity shall overwhelm thee, where the voice of joy and gladness shall be heard through all thy dwelling, and the voice of lamentation shall be heard no more. Then " why art thou cast down, O my soul? and why art thou disquieted within me? hope in God: for I shall yet praise him, who is the health of my countenance, and my God."

IX.—THE GOOD SAMARITAN.

" Cast thy burden on the Lord."—It is a blessed thing, O my soul, that thou art invited

to cast thy burden on the Lord—the burden of
thy fears, the burden of thy sorrows, the burden
of thy guilt; for thou canst not carry it thyself.
The weight of it is more than thou art able to
bear.   It is bowing thee down to the very dust,
and, left upon thine own shoulders, would ex-
haust thy strength, and sink thee down to the
lowest hell.   It is a blessed thing that thou art
invited to cast it upon the Lord; for He knows
the weight of it, and is well able to sustain it,
and is bowing down His own shoulders that you
may put it on.   Yet that is the great difficulty.
I would like to get rid of it.   I would fain relieve myself from the oppressive and insupport-
able load; but I am not able even to lift it up
and to cast it off.   I feel as if I were lying
prostrate, helpless, hopeless, spiritless, without
strength, devoid of all ability to help myself,
in the grasp of the mortal enemy, fainting,
worn out, ready to perish.   Oh, weary, deeply
wounded, broken - hearted, heavy - laden soul,
where can I look, whither can I go, what can I
find to meet the necessities of such a case, or to
assuage the griefs of a spirit so crushed with
anguish, and so despairing of relief?   I look
around, on the right hand and on the left, to see
if there be any help excepting the help that
comes from myself—any power from any quar-
ter, whether near or afar off, that is yet to be had

for a case apparently so desperate; and what is the result? I am driven out of myself. I am shut up to the necessity of looking only to the good Samaritan that is passing by. Though the weight of the burden has overmastered my strength, and crushed me down like a nether millstone, and left me lying amid the very dust of death, my only hope is in Him. But for Him I must perish, and perish everlastingly. But my waiting eyes are towards Him. It is from Him, and from Him alone, that my help cometh. It is He, and none but He, that is able to save even unto the uttermost. Of life, hope, strength, in myself there is none. But it hath pleased the Father that in Him all the fulness should dwell. In my helplessness I cast myself on His tender mercies. Oh, may He stoop down to relieve me of the burden which I can neither bear, nor lift up, nor cast off; and, instead of leaving me to sink beneath the weight, or vainly struggling to sustain it, may He lift it with His own hand, and transfer it to His own shoulders, giving me in exchange His own yoke which is easy, and His own burden which is very light.

X.—CHRIST'S DYING COMMAND.

" This do in remembrance of me."—What, O

my soul, does the loving Saviour ask or expect
at your hands at the communion table ? or what
are the words which drop from His gracious lips ?
His words are these, "Eat, O friends; drink, yea,
drink abundantly, O beloved." And why ? Is
it that He may enrich Himself at your expense?
that He may demand a price for the provisions
which you receive at His hands ? that He may
establish a claim for Himself on your money, or
your merits, or your promises, or anything what-
soever which you have in your possession, or
which you bring along with you to the table ?
No such thing. In point of fact, you have nothing which it is fit for Him to receive. All
that He asks is a remembrance of Himself—a
remembrance of His sovereign grace, a remembrance of His rich gifts, a remembrance of His
agonising sufferings, a remembrance of His finished work, a remembrance of His perfect righteousness all wrought out, and made ready, and
freely offered to your acceptance. Even when
sitting at the table, and eating the bread, and
drinking the wine, He does not seek to mar your
enjoyment, or to disturb your peace, by bringing
to your remembrance anything that relates to
yourself, anything that has to do with your past
sins, your grievous backslidings, your great pro-
vocations, your manifold infirmities, your languid affections, your distracting fears, your slow

progress, your unbelieving heart. Yourself, or anything connected with yourself, you are not asked to remember, excepting in so far as they lead you to look away from yourself, and to fix your undivided attention upon Him. It is enough for you if you are only careful to remember Christ—what He has said, what He has done, what He has suffered, what He has promised; and, losing sight of yourself, and remembering Him, and Him only, you will find, in the course of your personal experience, that by acting according to His counsel, a counsel as wise as it is gracious, you are taking the shortest road to the cross, where all your sins are nailed; to the treasury, where all your wants are provided for; to the grave, where all your griefs are buried; to the fountain, out of which all your consolations are drawn; and even to the open door in heaven, where, even now, you may catch, through the gilded openings of the darkest clouds, bright and seraphic visions of the glory that is yet to be revealed.

ACTION SERMON.

"Blessed are they which are called unto the marriage supper of the Lamb."—REV. xix. 9.

MANY blessings fall to the lot of the righteous, and these blessings follow them wherever they are, and whithersoever they go. Sometimes dark clouds may overshadow their path, floods of bitter tears may be falling from their eyes, and troubles great and manifold may be drinking up the oil of gladness out of their hearts; but still they are blessed. "Blessed are they that mourn, for they shall be comforted." Wicked men may speak peace to their own hearts, and wipe the tears from their own eyes, and hasten with accelerated steps to the broken cisterns whence they have been trying to draw water; but blessed, eminently blessed, are those mourners unto whom Christ bequeathes the legacy of peace, and whose tears have been wiped away by the hand of God.

At other times their spirits may be sorely amazed, brought down into the lowest depths,

encompassed with the horror of great darkness,
and, like Jonah in the days of old, their cry of
agony may seem as if it were coming up from
the belly of hell; for sins, innumerable as the
sands that lie scattered on the sea-shore, and
ponderous as the mountains that rise to the very
heavens, may be going over their heads, as a
heavy burden which they cannot bear, crushing
them down to the dust, and making them to feel
what a fearful thing it is to fall into the hands
of the living God. But, erelong, the raging
storm is changed into a great calm, and the
righteousness of the Divine Redeemer comes
rolling onwards, like the waves of the mighty
ocean, boundless, endless, and everlasting, hiding
millions of all monstrous and abominable iniquities from their view, swallowing up the very
sands of the sea-shore, as if it were invested
with the attributes of a living creature, and pro-
claiming, with a voice of grave and solemn
melody, " Blessed is the man whose transgression is forgiven, whose sin is covered, unto
whom the Lord imputeth not iniquity."

At another stage of their progress they may
be taken far away from the green pastures and
from beside the quiet waters, and conducted by a
strange and rugged path through the deep solitude, the overshadowing gloom, and the awful
horrors of the Valley of the Shadow of Death,

insomuch that the soul is ready to exclaim, " He hath led me, and brought me into darkness, but not into light. My flesh and my skin hath he made old ; he hath broken my bones. He hath builded against me, and compassed me with gall and travail. He hath also broken my teeth with gravel stones, he hath covered me with ashes. And thou hast removed my soul far off from peace: I forgat prosperity. And I said, My strength and my hope is perished from the Lord." But the light at eventide begins to shine. From the lowest depths the soul is still able to look up unto Him whence cometh its aid. Though far beyond the reach of human sympathy, the strength of an everlasting arm is felt to be round about and underneath. The stricken spirit, feeble and sore broken, has strength sufficient to articulate, ere it passes away, " Not alone ! not alone!" And when the languid eyelids close, and the accents of the faltering tongue give place to the stillness and solemnity of death, there is still a voice, and a voice that speaks of blessedness; but it comes from heaven—"Blessed are the dead which die in the Lord from henceforth: Yea, saith the Spirit, that they may rest from their labours ; and their works do follow them."

And then, when they have passed out of our sight altogether, and the places which they once occupied are left vacant, and we are inclined to weep over their removal with deep and poignant anguish, still we are not left to mourn as those that have no hope. They have only passed from a lower to a higher sphere, and, exchanging the grief for the glory, the trial for the triumph, and the cross for the crown, theirs now is a blessedness as everlasting in its duration as it is free from all alloy. "And he saith unto me, Write, Blessed are they which are called unto the marriage supper of the Lamb."

I. In the text reference is made, first of all, to a supper. What is the idea which this suggests? Observe, it is not a morning meal, preparatory to a long day of hard labour or of heavy trial. That, at least to the labouring man, is not the most fitting time either for pleasant fellowship or for quiescent enjoyment. His partner in life may be busily engaged with the necessary preparations. The little ones whom he loves so tenderly may still be sleeping quietly in their beds; and, perhaps, it may sometimes happen that he has scarcely set himself down at the breakfast table before the clock strikes, and the bell that summons him to his work is ringing loudly in his ears. It is a time, therefore, of haste, and of quick despatch, not of sweet and of tranquil rest. It is different with the supper— with the evening meal. The work of the day is then done. The burdened spirit is relieved, in a great measure, from the pressure of its cares; and the labouring man, laying aside his tools, and wiping the sweat from his brow, and casting off his soiled attire, comes home to his family to rest. If he be a man of sober habits, a stranger to the public-house, and a man of God, the Bible is brought out, the psalm is sung, the prayer is offered up, the board is spread, and he, and his wife, and his little ones, sit down together to the evening meal. It is a time of rest, of sweet fellowship, of joyous converse, perhaps the happiest hour of the day which the labouring man is permitted to enjoy. That is the first idea which we associate with the supper to which the text adverts. It speaks of rest, of quiescent enjoyment when the work of the day is done.

II. It is the Supper of the Lamb. Who is this? It is Christ, the Lamb of God, who taketh away the sin of the world, and whose blood cleanseth from all iniquity. It is not the labourer's supper; it is not his own providing, the reward of his own exertions, the fruit of his own toil. It is the Supper of his Lord and Master. The bread is His; the wine is His; the house is His; the servants are His; the wedding garments are His. It is the Lord's Supper, and it is the Lord Himself who has borne all the heat and burden of the day. But having finished the work, and made all things ready, He does not sit down at the table alone. The desires of His loving heart are going out for fellowship. He must have somebody to share the feast along with Him. If the rich and the great and the noble are ready to esteem Him lightly, and will have no communion with Him, He sends His messengers to the highways and the hedges, to the streets and lanes of the city, and even to the dens of deepest and of darkest infamy, to constrain the poor, and the helpless, and the lame, and the halt, and the blind, who have neither been labouring nor providing for themselves, to come first of all unto Himself, to buy of Him, even without money and without price, gold tried in the fire that they may be rich, and white raiment that they may be clothed, and eyesalve that they may see. And when they have come unto Himself, and put on the wedding garment He has provided, He invites them to come into His own house, and, with His banner of love and salvation over them, to sit down at the table which is not only covered with His own bounties, but at which He Himself is presiding.

III. It is a Marriage Supper, a festival of great joy, a special occasion which brings all the scattered members of the family together, and where there is not only fellowship with one another, but union with Christ, which, when once established, can never be dissolved. No man can be called to the Marriage Supper of the Lamb, or will ever be permitted to share in its bounties, without being by faith united unto Christ. Everything in regard both to his present comfort and his future glory depends on the fact of his being " in Christ Jesus." In Christ Jesus! It is a peculiar expression. It is very often used by the Apostle Paul in his epistles to the Churches. And while his words are few and well chosen, he repeats the idea with some slight variations not less than fifty times. Speaking of the people of God, or of those who are called to the Marriage Supper of the Lamb, what does he say of them? Are they chosen from the foundation of the world? It is in Christ Jesus. Are they called? It is in Christ Jesus. Are they baptized? It is in Christ Jesus. Are they made nigh? It is in Christ Jesus. Are they faithful brethren? It is in Christ Jesus. Are they made the righteousness of God? It is in Christ Jesus. Are they blessed with all spiritual blessings in heavenly places? It is in Christ Jesus. Are they pressing forward to the prize of the high calling of God? It is in Christ Jesus. Are they sealed with the Holy Spirit of promise? It is in Christ Jesus. Have they obtained salvation with eternal glory? It is in Christ Jesus.

Or, to change the form of the expression, they are crucified with Christ; they are dead with Christ; they are buried with Christ; they are quickened together with Christ; they are risen with Christ; they live together with Christ; they abide in Christ; they are rooted in Christ; they grow up into Christ; they walk with Christ; they reign with Christ.

And, still farther, they are light in the Lord; they are strong in the Lord; they rejoice in the Lord; they stand fast in the Lord; they die in the Lord. Even when their eyes close, and the dust of the grave covers them, they sleep in Jesus; and when their eyes open again, and the watches of the dark night are past, they appear with Jesus in glory, and so are they ever with the Lord. Once united they are never separated;—once His, they are His for ever.

IV. The blessedness of those who are called to the Marriage Supper of the Lamb. In attempting to point out wherein this blessedness consists, the first idea that suggests itself is this, that Christ Himself shall be there—there, in the very form that is most closely associated with the wonders of redeeming love—in the form of the Lamb of God, who taketh away the sins of the world, and in whose blood the robes of the saints have been washed and made white. This

H

of itself is the main element in the felicity of
heaven, Christ's personal presence; and that is
what every individual believer shall be privileged
to realise.   To be permitted to pass without
challenge through the gates into the celestial
city, to drink to the satisfaction of his largest
desires from the rivers of everlasting pleasure
that are flowing from the throne of God, to range
uncontrolled and at liberty amid the company
of the crowned seraphim over all the golden
pavements of heaven, were of itself a privilege,
the blessedness of which no tongue can tell, no
heart conceive.   But, oh! what a heaven of
heavens must it be for the once wretched and
abandoned prodigal, the vessel of wrath that
seemed fitted only for perdition, not only to be
rescued everlastingly from the burning flames
of hell, and safely housed within the diamond
walls of heaven, but to find himself sitting
down as a welcome guest at the same table with
the very Being who is seated amid the effulgence of the eternal throne, with the government of all eternity on His shoulders, and the
crowns of all heaven's glorified nobility at His
feet; to perceive, in the wounds that are still
apparent in His hands, and His bosom, and His
feet, the fountain of all His past consolations,
and of all His present blessedness, and of all His
coming glory; to recognise, amid the brilliant

glories that encircle Him, and the trains of ministering servants that are standing before Him, and the floods of adoration that are rising everlastingly around Him, the same loving, tender-hearted, and most compassionate Redeemer, that passed by him when he was lying in his blood and pollutions,—that threw the mantle of His lovingkindness over him, and sent forth His good Spirit to bind up his bleeding wounds, and to pour into them the balm of a healing medicine,—that led him and fed him all his life long, giving to him angels' food when he was passing through the wilderness, drawing for his refreshment rivers of living water from the flinty rock, regaling him amid the weariness of his earthly journey with clusters of grapes fetched from the vineyards of Canaan, and revealing to him, through the gilded openings of the darkest clouds, bright glimpses of the radiant land that lies beyond,—the faithful, the loving, the ever-present Jehovah, who met him by the way, and never left him till He had brought him into the brightness and the felicities of heaven ! Oh ! the blessedness of meeting again with such a friend, and finding Him unaltered and immutable, save in this, that His bleeding wounds are all healed, the travail of His soul is past, and the lacerations of the thorns are displaced by the radiance of the crown. Oh ! the blessedness of meeting Him in such a scene, amid the light, and the music, and the serenity of heaven, far remote from the turmoils and the distractions of this lower world, where the blessed inhabitant shall say no more, " I am sick," and all that dwell therein shall be forgiven their iniquity ; where the glories of the Saviour's character, no longer obscured by the dark and cloudy vail, shall be seen by the glorified soul without any of the doubts and suspicions that now cast such bitterness into the cup of his sweetest enjoyments ; where the infirmities of the frail body, which are so fitted to clog his immortal energies, and to oppress him with the languor of heaviness and grief, shall be left everlastingly amid the dust and the corruptions of the grave, from which the Saviour's power has raised him ; and the table which is covered with Heaven's richest bounties shall never be withdrawn.

It is different with the communion table here. It seems to have little of the aspect of a marriage supper, a festival of joy. And no wonder. Christ Himself is not visibly present. The Master of the feast seems, to the outward appearance, to be awanting ; and though He may be spiritually present, or present to the eye of faith, yet the faith itself is often so feeble, and the infirmities so manifold, and the causes of annoyance so numerous, and the clouds of sorrow so thick, that the comforts of the Saviour's presence may not be vividly realised.

In point of fact, the communicants are not always in a comfortable state of mind. One, perhaps, may be groaning under the weight of some heavy burden, another may be penetrated to the heart by the poisoned arrow of some deep conviction, another may be weighed down with the pressure of some overwhelming trial, another may be mourning under the severity of some irreparable bereavement, another may be walking under the shadow of some dark cloud.

Then, moreover, the tables are divided. We do not all see one another face to face, nor can we be certain that all that are sitting with us at the same table are really belonging to Christ's family. The precious, to a certain extent, may be mingled with the vile ; the tares may be growing along with the wheat.

And, still further, where is the table of communion at which we ever sit without suffering the pangs of bereavement, without missing some loving and beloved friend, who went along with us to the house of God, and sat with us side by side at the same table ? These are recollections which the human mind cannot shake off amid the solemnities of a communion table, and which the solemnities of a communion table are fitted to bring more powerfully over the heart. And

though it be a blessed thing for the desolate widow
to go there, and to find Christ to be a husband;
and for the homeless stranger to go there, and to
find Christ to be a stay; and for the solitary orphan to go there, and to find Christ to be a father;
yet, there is something in the feelings and necessities of these bleeding hearts, and these broken
families, dwelling, as they can scarcely fail to do,
on the memory of bygone days, which is almost
sure to open the flood-gates of the heart, and to
turn the table of communion from a joyful feast
into a place of silent and of solemn weeping.

At the Marriage Supper of the Lamb it shall
be different.   There the precious shall not only
be separated from the vile, but all the precious,
all the called, all the chosen, shall be together.
The whole family of the redeemed shall then
be complete.   Not one member of the body of
Christ shall be awanting.   Every mansion in
the kingdom shall be filled with its appropriate
tenant, and every seat at the table shall be occupied with its invited guest.

. Oh ! the blessedness of meeting with Christ,
and with all Christ's blessed family, amid the
glories of such a tranquil, unsuffering, undying
land,—the land where there are no faintings of
heart, no wasting of disease, no beds of sickness,
no ravages of death, nothing that can hurt, nothing that can offend, nothing that can destroy,

but where all is light, and purity, and peace, through the vast range of an interminable eternity.

Oh! what blessed meetings shall be there, what tokens of friendly recognition, what reviving of old associations, what glad hearts, and what radiant faces, when the grave shall restore all that we have now lost, and the broken bonds shall be again knit together, which neither sin, nor sorrow, nor death, shall ever break! How ravishing the prospect of such a meeting with the loving ones over whose graves we are now weeping, and that upon the shores of that tranquil world which death's dark waves can never touch! With what transport and ecstacy of spirit shall we then partake together of the provisions of that marriage supper that shall never be withdrawn!

And now, dear friends, let me ask, by way of application, Who are they who are called to the Marriage Supper of the Lamb, and to whom all this blessedness belongs? Is there any way whereby we can find this out? Most assuredly there is. It is embodied in the preceding verse. In that verse it is said, that " to her," that is, to the bride, to the Church of Christ, to each individual who is made ready for the marriage supper, and who is privileged to partake of it—" to her was granted that she should be arrayed in fine linen, clean and white ; for the fine linen is the righteousness of saints." It is that which constitutes both the title and the preparation for the Marriage Supper of the Lamb ; and there is something most encouraging in the fact, that the blessedness of the saints is resting upon such a ground. For, observe, that the fine linen in which they are arrayed has not been woven or wrought out by themselves. If it had, so far from being clean and white, it would, at the best, have been nothing better than filthy rags, not only insufficient to cover their nakedness, but in itself altogether polluted and unclean. But it is distinctly stated that the fine linen in which she was arrayed was granted unto her. It did not originally belong to her, nor did it come to her as an inheritance to which she had an independent title, nor was it purchased by her by means placed at her own disposal. It was granted. It was a gift, a free gift, a thing to which she had no right in herself, a thing for which she was indebted solely and exclusively to the sovereign, unmerited grace of the giver. And what is meant by this fine linen, so clean and white, which constitutes the righteousness of the saints, and by which they are made ready for the Marriage Supper of the Lamb ? It is nothing less than the righteousness of Christ Himself; a righteousness which is free from the slightest taint of pollution; a righteousness without a single flaw in it which is discoverable by the eye of Infinite purity; a righteousness which needs only to be granted to the guiltiest and the filthiest sinners that ever lived, to present them faultless before the presence of the Divine Majesty, and that even with exceeding joy. And, moreover, it is a gift which Christ gives even now. We need not to wait for its communication till we have finished our earthly course, and have actually entered within the vail. If we do not receive it before then we never can receive it at all. The Saviour's righteousness is offered to our acceptance even now, and, until we receive it and put it on, we are lying under the curse, and are utterly unclean. But the moment the righteousness of Christ is granted unto us, we stand, as it were, in Christ's stead. His infinite merit becomes ours. In Him, as the beloved of the Father, we stand accepted; and, just because we are in Him, there is unto us no condemnation.

Here, then, the solemn question remains for the consideration of every one of you,—Is this righteousness yours? Have you taken it on the terms in which it is offered to your acceptance, casting utterly away from you the filthy rags that appertain to yourselves, and, in the exercise of a simple faith, appropriating the merit

I

of Christ's finished and accepted work? If
you have, it matters not how poor may be the
raiment in which you are clothed. With Christ
put on, the palace doors are opened for your admission. You are entitled to take your place
among the ranks of the King's sons and daugh-
ters. You have the right of entry into the most
holy place. You have liberty of access to the
throne on which the King is sitting. And there
is not a blessing which Christ hath purchased
with His blood which you are not warranted to
claim as the lot of your inheritance. With Christ
dwelling in you, and you dwelling in Him, you
are as welcome to the Father's love, and as entitled to the riches of the Father's grace, and as
sure of the glories of the Father's kingdom, as is
Christ Himself. Your title and your standing
are the same. If He is beloved of the Father,
so are you. If He is without spot and blemish,
so are you. If all things are His, they are also
yours, for you are Christ's, and Christ is God's.

But if you have not put on Christ, and are not
clothed with His righteousness, what are you?
Though your feet were resting on pavements of
sapphire, though your bodies were attired in
cloth of gold, though your heads were glittering
with coronets of diamonds, you are still naked,
polluted, abandoned outcasts, lying under the
curse, and amenable to the righteous judgment

of God. Yet Christ is standing at the door, spreading out the riches of His unsearchable grace, and saying, even to the poor, and the wretched, and the blind, and the miserable, and the naked, " I counsel thee to buy of me gold tried in the fire, that thou mayest be rich ; and white raiment, that thou mayest be clothed, and that the shame of thy nakedness do not appear ; and anoint thine eyes with eyesalve, that thou mayest see"—" Behold, I stand at the door, and knock ; if any man hear my voice, and open the door, I will come in to him, and will sup with him, and he with me."

Dear friends, it is Christ that is now knocking, and the sinner, peradventure, refuses to open, though the marriage supper is provided, and the wedding garment is made ready, and the free and generous invitation is coupled with a promise which nothing but the revelations of an eternal world will enable us to understand—the promise of a seat upon His own throne. But this will not last for ever. If the offer is neglected and despised, it will be the sinner that will knock next—knock when it is too late, knock when the door is shut. But Christ, in His turn, and in righteous retribution, and in accordance with the warnings of His own faithful word, will refuse to open, be the knocking ever so loud, returning this only for an answer, " I know

you not whence ye are; depart from me, all
ye workers of iniquity"—" Because I have called, and ye refused; I have stretched out my
hand, and no man regarded; but ye have set at
nought all my counsel, and would none of my
reproof: I also will laugh at your calamity; I
will mock when your fear cometh; when your
fear cometh as desolation, and your destruction
cometh as a whirlwind; when distress and anguish cometh upon you. Then shall they call
upon me, but I will not answer; they shall seek
me early, but they shall not find me."

FENCING OF THE TABLES.

INTENDING communicants, according to the constitution of the Church to which it is your privilege to belong, it is the office of the officiating minister to set a fence around the communion table, to protect it from the approach of unworthy communicants, and thereby to guard them from the guilt and the danger of eating and drinking judgment to themselves. In the discharge of so important a duty —a duty which involves weighty responsibilities, and which is compassed with many difficulties— a great deal is left to the minister's own judgment and experience, and sometimes it may happen that the fences which he places around the sacred table are either so wide, that the most worldly and inconsistent are not prevented from getting in, or else they are so very narrow, that the most humble minded and the most sensitive feel themselves to be shut out; and thus, in both cases, the design of Christ in the ordinance may be rendered

of none effect. Instead, therefore, of expressing
my own mind in the matter, I wish to refer you
to the unerring standard, both of faith and of
practice, which the Bible furnishes; and the fence
to which I point you is the one which, of all
others, is the most authoritative and the most
sacred, for it is a fence that is erected by the
hand of God Himself.

With this view let me call your attention, first
of all, to what is written for your guidance under
the dispensation of the Law:—" And the Lord
said unto Moses, Go unto the people, and sanc-
tify them to-day and to-morrow, and let them
wash their clothes, and be ready against the
third day: for the third day the Lord will come
down in the sight of all the people upon mount
Sinai. And thou shalt set bounds unto the
people round about, saying, Take heed to yourselves, that ye go not up into the mount, or
touch the border of it: whosoever toucheth the
mount shall be surely put to death: there shall
not an hand touch it, but he shall surely be
stoned, or shot through; whether it be beast or
man, it shall not live: when the trumpet sound-
eth long, they shall come up to the mount"—
" And God spake all these words, saying, I am
the Lord thy God, which have brought thee out
of the land of Egypt, out of the house of bond-
age. Thou shalt have no other gods before me.

Thou shalt not make unto thee any graven image: or any likeness of anything that is in heaven above, or that is in the earth beneath, or that is in the water under the earth : thou shalt not bow down thyself to them, nor serve them : for I the Lord thy God am a jealous God, visiting the iniquity of the fathers upon the children unto the third and fourth generation of them that hate me ; and shewing mercy unto thousands of them that love me, and keep my commandments. Thou shalt not take the name of the Lord thy God in vain ; for the Lord will not hold him guiltless that taketh his name in vain. Remember the Sabbath day, to keep it holy. Six days shalt thou labour, and do all thy work: but the seventh day is the Sabbath of the Lord thy God: in it thou shalt not do any work, thou, nor thy son, nor thy daughter, thy manservant, nor thy maidservant, nor thy cattle, nor thy stranger that is within thy gates: for in six days the Lord made heaven and earth, the sea, and all that in them is, and rested the seventh day: wherefore the Lord blessed the Sabbath day, and hallowed it. Honour thy father and thy mother: that thy days may be long upon the land which the Lord thy God giveth thee. Thou shalt not kill. Thou shalt not commit adultery. Thou shalt not steal. Thou shalt not bear false witness against thy neighbour. Thou shalt not covet thy neighbour's house, thou shalt not covet thy neighbour's wife, nor his manservant, nor his maidservant, nor his ox, nor his ass, nor anything that is thy neighbour's" (Exod. xix. 10–13, and xx. 1–17). Thus it was under the dispensation that is past.

Let me next advert to what is written for your guidance under the dispensation of the Gospel: —" Brethren, ye have been called unto liberty ; only use not liberty for an occasion to the flesh, but by love serve one another. For all the law is fulfilled in one word, even in this ; Thou shalt love thy neighbour as thyself. But if ye bite and devour one another, take heed that ye be not consumed one of another. This I say then, Walk in the Spirit, and ye shall not fulfil the lust of the flesh. For the flesh lusteth against the Spirit, and the Spirit against the flesh : and these are contrary the one to the other ; so that ye cannot do the things that ye would. But if ye be led by the Spirit, ye are not under the law. Now the works of the flesh are manifest, which are these ; Adultery, fornication, unclean- ness, lasciviousness, idolatry, witchcraft, hatred, variance, emulations, wrath, strife, seditions, heresies, envyings, murders, drunkenness, re- vellings, and such like : of the which I tell you before, as I have also told you in time past, that they which do such things shall not inherit the kingdom of God. But the fruit of the Spirit is love, joy, peace, long-suffering, gentleness, goodness, faith, meekness, temperance : against such there is no law. And they that are Christ's have crucified the flesh with the affections and lusts" (Gal. v. 13–24). " This I say therefore, and testify in the Lord, that ye henceforth walk not as other Gentiles walk, in the vanity of their mind, having the understanding darkened, being alienated from the life of God through the ignorance that is in them, because of the blindness of their heart: who being past feeling have given themselves over unto lasciviousness, to work all uncleanness with greediness. But ye have not so learned Christ ; if so be that ye have heard him, and have been taught by him, as the truth is in Jesus : that ye put off concerning the former conversation the old man, which is corrupt according to the deceitful lusts; and be renewed in the spirit of your mind ; and that ye put on the new man, which after God is created in righteousness and true holiness. Wherefore putting away lying, speak every man truth with his neighbour : for we are members one of another. Be ye angry, and sin not : let not the sun go down upon your wrath : neither give place to the devil. Let him that stole steal no more : but rather let him labour, working with his hands the thing which is good, that

K

he may have to give to him that needeth. Let
no corrupt communication proceed out of your
mouth, but that which is good to the use of edi-
fying, that it may minister grace unto the
hearers. And grieve not the Holy Spirit of
God, whereby ye are sealed unto the day of redemption. Let all bitterness, and wrath, and
anger, and clamour, and evil speaking, be put
away from you, with all malice: and be ye kind
one to another, tender-hearted, forgiving one
another, even as God for Christ's sake hath forgiven you" (Eph. iv. 17–32). Thus it is under
the dispensation that is present.

And observe, finally, what is written for your
guidance under the dispensation that is yet to
come:—" And I saw a new heaven and a new
earth: for the first heaven and the first earth
were passed away; and there was no more sea.
And I John saw the holy city, new Jerusalem,
coming down from God out of heaven, prepared
as a bride adorned for her husband. And I
heard a great voice out of heaven saying, Behold, the tabernacle of God is with men, and
he will dwell with them, and they shall be his
people, and God himself shall be with them,
and be their God. And God shall wipe away
all tears from their eyes; and there shall be no
more death, neither sorrow, nor crying, neither
shall there be any more pain: for the former

things are passed away. And he that sat upon the throne said, Behold, I make all things new. And he said unto me, Write: for these words are true and faithful. And he said unto me, It is done. I am Alpha and Omega, the beginning and the end. I will give unto him that is athirst of the fountain of the water of life freely. He that overcometh shall inherit all things; and I will be his God, and he shall be my son. But the fearful, and unbelieving, and the abominable, and murderers, and whoremongers, and sorcerers, and idolaters, and all liars, shall have their part in the lake which burneth with fire and brimstone: which is the second death "—" And, behold, I come quickly; and my reward is with me, to give every man according as his work shall be. I am Alpha and Omega, the beginning and the end, the first and the last. Blessed are they that do his commandments, that they may have right to the tree of life, and may enter in through the gates into the city. For without are dogs, and sorcerers, and whoremongers, and murderers, and idolaters, and whosoever loveth and maketh a lie " (Rev. xxi. 1-8, and xxii. 12-15).

A threefold cord is not easily snapped asunder, and a threefold fence is not easily broken down; and such is the fence which God Himself has erected. You have it under the dispensation

that is past; you have it under the dispensation that is present; you have it under the
dispensation that is yet to come; and the fence
is in every case inscribed with these words,
" Holiness unto the Lord." That is the badge
which is written on the Law, the badge which is
written on the Gospel, the badge which is written on the gates of heaven. Wherever God is to
be approached,—whether on the mercy-seat, or
the golden altar, or the communion table, or the
throne of judgment—we are to draw near with
reverent steps, with clean hands, with anointed
lips, with pure hearts. Mount Sinai, with its
thunders and its clouds of darkness; Mount
Calvary, with its cross and its mortal agonies;
Mount Zion, with its harps, and its angelic
hosts, and its golden crowns, are every one of
them guarded against the approach of ungodly
men. May it be given to each intending communicant, by the Spirit that cometh down from
above, to mark the fences which God Himself
has erected, carefully and reverently to read the
notices which God has hung up in the face of
open day, and, instead of impiously attempting
to break down the sacred barriers, and earning
the punishment of men that are trespassing on
forbidden ground, may it be your blessed privilege to have both the name and the character
of His children, that, bearing His image, and

clothed in the beauties of holiness, you may enter without challenge by the door which He Himself hath opened, and may sit down, with the freedom that belongs to the family, with a hearty welcome from the Father's loving heart, at the table which His own hands have spread, and at which He Himself is presiding.

ADDRESSES AT THE TABLE.

I.—THE BROKEN SPIRIT.

COMMUNICANTS, I have read of a poor Jew who came up to worship before the Lord, having just risen from a sickbed, where he had lingered for many months, longing and panting for the courts of the Lord. It was with difficulty that he could sustain his tottering limbs, yet, mingling with the multitude that kept holyday, he entered into the Lord's house to witness the morning sacrifice. The words of the Psalmist fell upon his ear like the music of some celestial melody, "Thou desirest not sacrifice; else would I give it: thou delightest not in burnt offering. The sacrifices of God are a broken spirit: a broken and a contrite heart, O God, thou wilt not despise." The service proceeded. One after another brought his offering, and was accepted, and went away again to his own home. But the poor invalid had nothing to present. Nevertheless, he lingered within the courts of the Lord's house, reluctant to leave, without a blessing, the sacred place where the name of God was recorded, yet holding back to the very last, as if he felt himself to be the least of all saints, or else the chiefest of all sinners. At length he ventured to draw near, and fell down with his face to the ground before the officiating priest. "What wilt thou, my son," said the venerable man; "hast thou an offering?" "No, my father," said the poor penitent, "a desolate widow and her fatherless children came to me in great straits, and I had nothing to give them but the two young pigeons which were ready for the sacrifice." "Bring, then," the priest replied, "an ephah of fine flour, and thy gift shall be accepted on the altar of God." "Nay, my father," the poor penitent replied, "this day my sickness and my poverty left me barely enough for my famishing children. I have not even an ephah of flour." "Wherefore, then, comest thou hither? Thou hast no offering. What is the burden of thy request? Is there ought that I, the minister of God, can yet do for thee?" The poor penitent replied, "When I entered the courts of the Lord's house I heard them singing, 'The sacrifices of God are a broken spirit: a broken and a contrite heart, O God, thou

wilt not despise.' That is all that I have to offer.
God be merciful to me the sinner."

The old priest was melted. The tear started
into his eye. He lifted up the feeble and ema-
ciated mourner from the ground. He laid his
hand upon his head, and pronounced the cheering benediction, "Blessed art thou, my son,
thine offering is accepted. It is better than
thousands of rivers of oil. Jehovah, that dwelleth between the cherubim, bless thee; Jehovah
be gracious unto thee, and make His face to
shine upon thee; Jehovah lift up the light of
His countenance upon thee, and give thee peace."

Communicants, after all your searchings of
heart, your waiting upon instituted ordinances,
your fervent longings for the communications
of the Holy Spirit, have you found nothing to
present unto God,—no gift, no grace, no faith,
no penitence, no love, not even the smallest of
offerings—the two pigeons, the widow's mite,
the ephah of flour? Nevertheless, your case is
not hopeless. Better go to the well of Samaria
with an empty pitcher, panting and thirsting
for the living water, than sit down at the feast
of fat things with a full soul, that is loathing
even the sweetness of the honeycomb. And be
not greatly disheartened, at least if there be
within you a broken spirit. There are blessings
sometimes connected with things that are

broken. It is the broken rock that sends forth the streams of living water through the wilderness; the broken ground which, receiving the precious seed, brings forth in some thirty, in some sixty, and in some an hundred fold; the broken alabaster, with whose ointment poured forth the poor penitent anoints the feet of the Saviour, and which fills the whole house with the odour of the precious spikenard; the broken body, which the rough nails of the cross and the spear of a mortal enemy have pierced, which supplies the blood which cleanses the soul from all sin; the broken grave, which announces the reality of the resurrection, and proclaims to the unbelieving disciple that the Saviour is risen indeed; the broken vail that opens into the holiest of all, and gives to the believing soul bright glimpses into the glory that is yet to be revealed; the broken bread on the sacramental table, which, fraught with the Saviour's blessing, brings life and spirit unto the soul; the broken fruit from the vineyards and olive groves of Canaan, which, crushed by the ponderous millstone, makes the lamps of the tabernacle to shine, or which, trodden in the winepress and treasured up in earthen vessels, ripens into the wine of Lebanon; and it is the broken and the contrite spirit that the Lord will not despise. " Thus saith the high and lofty One that in-

habiteth eternity, whose name is Holy; I dwell
in the high and holy place, with him also that
is of a contrite and humble spirit, to revive the
spirit of the humble, and to revive the heart of
the contrite ones."

II.—THE WEDDING GARMENT.

" I will greatly rejoice in the Lord, my soul
shall be joyful in my God; for he hath clothed
me with the garments of salvation, he hath
covered me with the robe of righteousness, as
a bridegroom decketh himself with ornaments,
and as a bride adorneth herself with her jewels."
—Communicants, this is the utterance of a soul
prepared for sitting down at the table of the
Lord—the utterance of a soul made ready for
the Marriage Supper of the Lamb; for observe
whither it is that the faith of such a soul is looking, and whence it is that the joy of such a soul
is flowing forth—" I will greatly rejoice in the
Lord, my soul shall be joyful in my God." The
man is not looking to anything inherent in himself, nor going about for the establishment of a
righteousness of his own, nor even resting with
a feeling of complacency on the strength and

efficacy of his own faith. His eye is looking
in another direction. All his well-springs are
in Christ. It is in the Lord Jehovah that he
has righteousness and strength. And it is just
because he is looking away from his own emptiness to Christ's fulness ; from his own poverty
to Christ's riches ; from his own rags to Christ's
righteousness ; from his own pollutions to
Christ's cleansing blood ; from his own weakness to Christ's never-failing strength ; from his
own misery to Christ's boundless consolations,
that he finds vent to his feelings in the beautiful language of the prophet, " I will greatly
rejoice in the Lord, my soul shall be joyful in
my God."

But whilst the believing soul looks directly
unto God through Christ, and finds in Him the
perennial sources of his consolation and his joy,
he takes also a glance at himself, and what does
he find there ? " He hath clothed me with the
garments of salvation, he hath covered me with
the robe of righteousness, as a bridegroom decketh himself with ornaments, and as a bride
adorneth herself with her jewels."

The man is not now lying in the open wilderness, in his blood and in his pollutions. The
Saviour has passed by him, and has cast His
mantle over him. The wretched prodigal is no
longer feeding upon the husks, and lingering

amid the swineherds of the far distant land. He has crossed the threshold of his Father's house; the shoes are upon his feet; the ring is upon his finger; the feast of fat things is prepared; the best robe is around him, and therefore he is warranted to exclaim, " I will greatly rejoice in the Lord, my soul shall be joyful in my God; for he hath clothed me with the garments of salvation, he hath covered me with the robe of righteousness, as a bridegroom decketh himself with ornaments, and as a bride adorneth herself with her jewels."

It is one thing for the naked and polluted soul, still lying in its blood, to know that the garment of salvation is provided, and is offered to its acceptance, even though as yet it should be laid up in the repositories of Christ's wardrobe. It is another thing when the garment of salvation is brought forth, and wrapt around him, when he feels the comfort of it, when he knows it to be his own. This is the doing of the Lord, and it is wonderful in his eyes : God not only provides the garment of salvation, but He puts it on; and being put on, the soul rejoices and is made glad.

Is it so with you, communicants, and is that the point of which you wish to be assured ? Then here is the test. The man whom God clothes with the garment of salvation, He also covers with the robe of righteousness. Both are provided, and both are indispensable. By means of the one, the garment of salvation, he is brought into a state of safety; he is delivered from the sentence of condemnation; he acquires a title to the blessedness of heaven. By means of the other, the robe of righteousness, he is brought into a state of holiness; the strength of indwelling corruption is subdued; he is changed into the likeness of the Divine image; he is made meet and made ready for sitting down for ever at the Marriage Supper of the Lamb.

The one is the work of Christ; the other is the work of the Spirit; and the believing soul, sharing in them both, may well exclaim at the sacred table, "I will greatly rejoice in the Lord, my soul shall be joyful in my God; for he hath clothed me with the garments of salvation, he hath covered me with the robe of righteousness, as a bridegroom decketh himself with ornaments, and as a bride adorneth herself with her jewels."

III.—THE WELL OF BETHLEHEM.

It is said of David, when he was lodged in the

rock at the cave of Adullam, and when the
Philistines were pitched in the plains of Re-
phaim, that he longed fervently, and said, " Oh
that one would give me to drink of the water of
the well of Bethlehem, which is by the gate !
And three mighty men brake through the host
of the Philistines, and drew water out of the
well, and brought it to David: nevertheless he
would not drink thereof, but poured it out unto
the Lord. And he said, Be it far from me, O
Lord, that I should do this : is not this the blood
of the men that went in jeopardy of their lives ?
therefore he would not drink it," but poured it
out unto the Lord, thereby turning it from a
common to a sacred use, and regarding it, by
virtue of the blood with which it had been
procured, as if it were a holy or a consecrated
thing.

Communicants, what is the feeling which
this striking incident is fitted to awaken in
your minds ? You may have fled to your
stronghold, like the prisoners of hope, yet, like
David in the rock at the cave of Adullam, you
may become faint and weary in your minds,
and may, therefore, be prompted to exclaim,
" Oh that one would give me to drink, not of
the well of Bethlehem, nor of the streams that
issue from any broken cistern ; but, oh that one
would give me to drink of the wells of salva-

tion, the streams of the river that maketh glad the city of our God, the water of the well of Lebanon."

That is what you need, and what you cannot do without. And if you set your heart upon it, and ask it in faith, you are sure to get it, to get it as often and as abundantly as your need may be. But let me remind you that it was a deep well out of which Christ had to draw it. He had to go far down in the scale of His humiliation, even to the lowest possible point, before He could reach it; and ere one drop of that living water could be obtained for you, He had to fight His way through the abominations of a fallen world, and through the floods of ungodly men, and through the thick and embattled ranks of the mightiest powers and principalities of hell. Yet it is offered to you freely. You are made welcome to take it. You have nothing to pay for it. The price is already paid, paid to the last farthing, paid by blood, most precious blood, the blood which all the wealth of this boundless universe can never estimate— the blood of Christ's broken heart. Take care, therefore, that you never think lightly of it, nor trample it beneath your feet as if it were a common or an unholy thing. But while you make full trial of its cleansing virtue, and rejoice in the plenitude of its Divine consolations,

look also to the hole, of the rock from which it
has been drawn, and remembering the enor-
mous price that has been paid for it, and con-
secrating yourselves, with all that you have,
unto the Lord, who hath redeemed you with
His own blood, let yours be the language of the
prophet, of old, " O Lord I will praise thee:
though thou wast angry with me, thine anger
is turned away, and thou comfortedst me. Behold, God is my salvation ; I will trust, and not
be afraid : for the Lord Jehovah is my strength
and my song; he also is become my salvation.
Therefore with joy shall ye draw water out of
the wells of salvation."

IV.—THE CLIFT IN THE ROCK.

When Moses went into the tabernacle of the
congregation to intercede for the children of
Israel, we are told that the cloudy pillar, the
symbol of the Divine presence, descended and
stood, not at a great distance away from him, or
far up in the serene firmament of heaven, but at
the door of the tabernacle, wherein the Lord was
about to converse with him face to face. And
we are told, moreover, that all the people rose
up, and looked after Moses, and worshipped

every man in his tent door. And what was the result of this communion on the part of Moses within the tabernacle of the congregation, followed up and associated as it was with the exercises of religious worship on the part of all Israel, every man joining in the devotions, and bowing himself down in spirit before God at his tent door? The result was this:—Moses found grace in the sight of the Lord, and God not only engaged that His presence would go with him, and that He would give him rest, but He promised to shew him His glory, saying unto him, " Thou canst not see my face : for there shall no man see me, and live. But, behold, there is a place by me, and thou shalt stand upon a rock : and it shall come to pass, while my glory passeth by, that I will put thee in a clift of the rock, and will cover thee with my hand while I pass by."

Now observe, communicants, by what means this remarkable promise was obtained. It was obtained in answer to prayer—prayer on the part of the children of Israel in their tents, and prayer on the part of Moses within the tabernacle of the congregation that was without the camp. But where was it that the promise was fulfilled ? Not in the tents of Israel, nor even in the tabernacle of the congregation, but Moses was commanded to make himself ready, and to come up in the morning unto mount Sinai, and to present

M

himself before God on the top of the mount.
And it was while he was there, in the clear light
of the morning, when the freshness of heaven
was around him, when the dark shadows of the
night had departed, and when he was alone with
God, abstracted from the concerns of this lower
world, and lifted to an immeasurable elevation
above the tents of Israel, that the Lord descended
in a cloud, and stood with him there, and put
him in the clift of the rock, and covered him in
the hollow of His hand, and proclaimed the
name of the Lord;—" The Lord, the Lord God,
merciful and gracious, longsuffering, and abundant in goodness and truth, keeping mercy for
thousands, forgiving iniquity, and transgression,
and sin."

And what was the result ?   When Moses
came down from the mount, where he had been
conversing with God, he carried in his own person the palpable and incontestable evidences
that he had seen somewhat of His glory.   Even
though he had been put into the clift of the rock
while God was passing by, nevertheless the light
was so penetrating, and the radiance was so refulgent, as to change him into the likeness of the
same image.   And when he mingled with the
hosts of Israel his face was shining, and the
brightness was so dazzling that they could not
look upon him ; they were afraid to come near

him ; and, in order to re-establish their confidence and to invite their approach, he was
under the necessity of putting a veil upon his
face, to soften down the insufferable glory, and
to convince them, that while he was talking
with them he was still clothed in the humanity
of their own nature, and was a man of like
passions with themselves.

Communicants, if you have been much exercised in prayer in your tents or your dwellings,
and, like Israel of old, have risen up with one
consent, and, with united hearts and with earnest
supplications, have been looking after the ministers of God when they were going, for your sakes,
into the courts of the Lord's house, then, in that
case, I do not doubt that, when seated at the table
of communion, or carried up to the top of the
mount, the Lord Himself will hold communion
with you, putting you into the clift of the rock,
and, amid the proclamation of His great name,
and the passing by of His glory, prompting you
to exclaim,—

" Rock of Ages, cleft for me, let me hide myself in Thee—
Let the water and the blood, from Thy riven side that flow'd,
Be of sin the double cure, cleanse me from its guilt and power.
Rock of Ages, cleft for me, let me hide myself in Thee."

And when you descend from the mount, or leave
the table of communion, see that you shew by
the shining of your countenances where it is

that you have been, and what it is that you have
been doing. Take care that you bring not an
evil name on the holy religion which you profess
by the gross and palpable inconsistency of your
conduct. Beware of casting a stumblingblock
in the way of other men, or among the members
of your own households, or in the view of your
domestic servants, by your hasty language, or
your forbidding looks, or your ill-regulated tempers, or your rash judgments, or your unholy
deportment. Instead of this, let all wrath, and
anger, and clamour, and bitterness, and malice,
and evil speaking, be put away from you. And
should there be no enterprise of Christian bene-
ficence upon which you can enter, or no good
service that you can render to the humblest of
your brethren of mankind, oh see, at all events,
that there be something in the outbursting
lovingkindness of your hearts, and in the be-
nignant shining of your very faces, that will
diffuse so genial an atmosphere around you as
may have the effect of dissipating the prejudices
of worldly men, and leading them to think well
of the loving Redeemer at whose table you have
been sitting, and whose love has been shed
abroad upon your hearts.

V.—THE GARDEN OF SPICES.

In walking through the vineyards and orange groves of another and a brighter land than this, I have been much impressed, not more by the sight of the green foliage, and the graceful forms of the fruit bearing trees, than by the sweetness of the incense which the soft winds were instrumental in drawing out from the expanding blossoms and the golden fruit. When the atmosphere was perfectly calm, and the trees were utterly at rest, there was still the same beauty, and the same bright and abundant fruit; but whenever the wind awoke, and began to play amongst the branches, it was then especially that the whole atmosphere was filled with fragrancy, which, whilst most grateful to the senses, went up sweetly, but silently, unto heaven. The fresh impression which I now entertain of those fruitful groves, and those aromatic odours, forcibly suggests, as a subject suitable for meditation and devotion at the table of communion, these words from the Song of Solomon, "Awake, O north wind, and come, thou south, blow upon my garden, that the spices thereof may flow out. Let my beloved come into his garden, and eat his pleasant fruits."

Communicants, this brings vividly before you
a consideration in regard to the sacred ordinance
which you may be apt to exclude, in a great
measure, from your thoughts. You may feel
that it is an ordinance by means of which you
are invited to enter into fellowship with Christ,
but you may not feel in the same way that it is
an ordinance also by means of which Christ purposes to enter into fellowship with you. Your
desires may be going out towards Him, and towards the remembrance of His name, that so
you may find Him to be the chiefest of ten
thousand, and altogether lovely; but you may
not be fully alive to the precious consideration
that the desires of Christ are going out with
equal earnestness towards you, that so He may
see of the travail of His soul, and be satisfied.
'You may be perfectly aware that it is a right
and proper thing on your part to be waiting at
the posts of Christ's door, asking that you may
receive, seeking that you may find, knocking
that it may be opened to you; but you may not
clearly perceive that Christ, on the other hand,
is standing, with equal urgency and importunity,
at the door of your hearts, standing there till
His head is filled with dew, and His locks with
the drops of the night, putting the hands, that
are dropping with myrrh, on the handles of the
lock, and saying, with a voice that is full of

tenderness, " Behold, I stand at the door, and knock ; if any man hear my voice, and open the door, I will come in to him, and will sup with him." It is one thing for you to have an open door into Christ's fulness and all-sufficiency, that, all your well-springs being in Him, you may be filled with joy unspeakable and full of glory ; but it is another thing for Christ to have an open door into the innermost recesses of your own hearts, that so He may come in, and remain there as an abiding guest, and not as a stranger and wayfaring man that turneth aside to tarry only for a night. It is not enough that Christ be held forth to you as the rose of Sharon, as the lily of the valleys, as the apple tree among the trees of the wood, that so you may sit under His shadow with great delight, and His fruit may be sweet unto your taste ; but it is befitting that you, on the other hand, should be held forth to Christ as an orchard of pomegranates, with all trees of frankincense, and all pleasant fruits, with saffron and spikenard, and myrrh and cinnamon.

For that purpose, communicants, both the north wind and the south must be made to blow upon you,—the north wind, with its withering frosts and its chilling blasts, to kill, and to keep down, and to root up whatever is fitted to hurt, or to offend, or to destroy ; and the south wind,

with its balmy gales and its genial showers, to
expand the bright blossoms, to mature the precious fruit, and to cause the aromatic spices to
flow out. Without that there can be no beauty,
no vitality, no growth. All will be cold, dead,
sterile, unprofitable ; no manifestation of the
graces which it is the office of the Divine Spirit
to nourish; no appearance of the fruit which it
is the pleasure of the Divine Redeemer to gather.
Yet that is the very thing which Christ looks
for, and which He has a right to expect. If,
therefore, you are summoned to enter into vital
fellowship with Him, it is to bring you into a
condition where your joy shall not only be full,
but where your fruit shall be abundant. For
herein is your Father glorified, that ye bring
forth much fruit. Oh see, then, that ye keep
this in view, that instead of being like a garden
enclosed, or a fountain sealed up, you may become what it is the design of the Saviour's grace
to make you—a fruitful vineyard, a well of living
water, and streams from Lebanon, spreading
health and vitality on all that are round about
you, and so causing the spices to flow forth, that
men may not only take knowledge of you that
you have been with Christ, but that Christ Himself may come into His garden, and eat of His
pleasant fruit.

VI.—THE ROYAL GALLERIES.

In the Song of Solomon the great Redeemer is set before His believing people in the character of a king, wearing the diadem with which He was crowned in the day of His espousals, bringing them into the banqueting house, over which the banner of love has been spread, and saying unto them, " Eat, O friends ; drink, yea, drink abundantly, O beloved." And there are some occasions in which He is so attracted with the graces of His people, or with the earnest desires and the warm affections which He Himself has implanted, that He cannot get away, and hence the remarkable expression, " The king is held in the galleries."

That I reckon to be the high and holy place, the place of audience, the council chamber, where He is encompassed with the insignia of royalty, where He sits upon the throne and the mercy-seat to receive the petitions of His people, to load them with the riches of His liberality, and to make them glad with His royal favour.

But He is not always in the galleries, or in the banqueting house, or at the table. Sometimes He is in the wilderness, or in the gardens, or among the beds of spices, or in the broadways

N

of the city, or on the mountains of Bether, or in the vineyards of Engedi, or standing behind the wall, or shewing Himself at the lattice, or knocking at the outer door, or putting His fingers on the handles of the lock, or in the secret places of the stairs.   But wherever He may be, if you, communicants, are seeking Him, and following hard after Him, it is so far well.   It is well to be seeking for Him amid the dark watches of the night, in the streets and broadways of the city, and saying earnestly to the watchmen, "Saw ye him whom my soul loveth?"   It is well to be looking out for Him, even as one looketh out for the dawning of the morning, when He cometh out of the wilderness, perfumed with frankincense, and leaping upon the mountains of Bether.   It is well to be meeting Him with a cordial welcome when He appeareth from behind the wall, or sheweth Himself at the lattice.   It is well to be standing ready for the opening of the door, when the sweet smelling myrrh is dropping from the handles of the lock, and the soft and gentle voice of your Beloved is saying, "Open unto me; for my head is filled with dew, and my locks with the drops of the night."   It is well to have your heart's desires going out earnestly towards Him, even from the lowest depths, or from the secret places of the stairs.

But if you would sit down with the King at

His table, and behold Him in His regal majesty, you must lay aside your filthy attire, and put off the dusty shoes from your feet, and turn from the turmoils of this sordid world, and, taking with you the wedding garment, and the new name, and the white stone, you must leave the outer and the lower courts, and go up till you find yourselves in the royal apartments, in the very galleries of the King; for it is there that the King is held, that He is detained, that He is prevented from getting away. And wherefore, or how long? Till every petition has been presented, every case has been considered, every claim has been adjusted, every grievance has been redressed, every want has been supplied, every doubt has been dispelled, every sorrow has been soothed, every blessing has been dispensed —until the feast has not only been spread in the banqueting house, but until the latest guest has risen from the table, and the neediest soul has been relieved from the pressure of every burden, and satisfied to the full with the joys of His great salvation.

Communicants, is it so with you? Have you gone up to the high and holy place? Have you seen the King in His majesty and glory? Have you presented your petition and obtained the answer? Have you been sitting with Him at the table, like king's sons, feasting on royal bounties, and having power to plead with Him, and to prevail? Then, how does it become you to feel and to act? When you come down from the royal galleries, and return, as heretofore, to the toils and the distractions of your worldly avocations, oh, see that you comport yourselves with the dignity and the elevation of spirit that is accordant with your ennobling privileges and your high rank. In all that you say, and in all that you do, let it be apparent that you are indeed " a chosen generation, a royal priesthood, an holy nation, a peculiar people ; that ye should shew forth the praises of him who hath called you out of darkness into his marvellous light." And, keeping your garments undefiled, and the lustre of your Christian graces unstained, let all men see, by the purity of your lives, and the consistency of your walk, and the heavenliness of your spirits, that you are " the sons of God without rebuke, in the midst of a crooked and perverse nation, among whom ye shine as lights in the world."

VII.—MOUNT PISGAH.

When Moses had pronounced his final blessing on the tribes of Israel, and had concluded the solemn benedictions with these beautiful words, "Happy art thou, O Israel: who is like unto thee, O people saved by the Lord"! we are led to understand that he went up from the plains of Moab, and ascended to the top of Pisgah, that is over against Jericho, and there he was admitted to the enjoyment of a high and distinguished privilege.   It was not, indeed, permitted him to pass over Jordan, and, along with the people with whom he had been so long and closely associated, to go up and to take possession of the promised land—the land that was flowing with milk and honey, and which was the glory of all lands.   God had reserved some better thing for him, and, instead of regaling him with the honey and the grapes of the earthly Canaan, He was purposing to remove him, and that very speedily, into the better and more enduring rest that remains for the people of God in heaven. He had already offered up the earnest prayer, "O Lord God, I pray thee, let me go over, and see the good land that is beyond Jordan, that goodly mountain, and Lebanon."   And that prayer was heard—not, indeed, very literally, nor in the way, perhaps, which Moses himself may have desired, but substantially, and in a way that was far better for himself; for God said unto him, "Let it suffice thee; speak no more unto me of this matter; for thou shalt not go over this Jordan;

but get thee up into the top of Pisgah, and lift up
thine eyes westward, and northward, and south-
ward, and eastward, and behold it with thine
eyes." Accordingly, this venerable man of God,
having finished his earthly labours, and pronounced his last blessing on Israel, turns his
footsteps from the camp which he had so long
directed with his counsels, and begins, solitary
and alone, to ascend into the hill of God, and
never halts, in that last and solemn journey,
till he gains the very summit, far up amid the
clouds of heaven; and when he looks around, and
underneath, and beyond him, what does he see?
On the one hand, and far below him, he beholds
the white tents of Israel, glittering in the distant sunbeams, the people safe now from the
vengeance of all their enemies, delivered from
the perils of the waste howling wilderness, Jehovah, the Lord of hosts, claiming them as the
lot of His own inheritance, preparing to lead
them over Jordan into the promised land, and
Himself going before them with the pillar of
cloud to guide them by day, and the pillar of
fire to give them light by night. And when he
looks before him and around him, what are the
objects that meet his gaze? Mount Lebanon,
embellished with its glorious cedars, and fragrant with its fruitful vines, lifting its everlasting head unto the heavens; and the whole land

which God had promised to Abraham, and Isaac, and Jacob, lying in all its rich and gorgeous magnificence before him. It was a glorious spectacle. Doubtless his whole soul was lifted up and transported with the sight; and, satisfied with the proofs which he had now obtained of the Divine faithfulness, and with the distant view of what God had provided for His people, he laid himself down, and, closing his eyes on the glories of the earthly Canaan, he passed within the vail, and, in a moment suddenly, was enshrined amid the splendours of heaven.

Communicants, the table of communion is meant to lead you up, as it were, from the plains of Moab, and from the summit of mount Pisgah, to give unto you the distant prospect of the promised land, the first-fruits and the foretaste of the felicities of heaven. But these are prospects which you can never see, and first-fruits which you can never taste, if you are abiding in the plains that are below, or dwelling in the tents of ungodly men. If you would catch even a distant glimpse of the glories of Lebanon, and carry your prospects over and beyond the dark swellings of Jordan, you must mount up, as upon the wings of an eagle, to the elevation of a higher region, and from the top of Pisgah, and with the eye of faith, and in communion with the glorified Redeemer, and through the power of the eternal Spirit, you must look as those who are strangers and pilgrims here unto the bright and the blessed land that lies beyond. And when you have infefted yourselves in the riches of its promised and purchased pos- sessions, it matters not though you should never come down to the plains of Moab, or seat your- selves at the communion table again—though, like Moses, you should cast off the mortal taber- nacle, and pass from the mount of communion to the seraphic visions of a higher world, or into the stupendous and unimaginable glories of heaven. But if you are permitted to come down, let yours be the language and the spirit of Canaan, let your conversation and your citizenship be in heaven, and, instead of mingling in the abomi- nations of the world, or following after vanity and lies, see that you comport yourselves as the children of the light and the day, that all around you may be led to glorify your Father who is in heaven, and that when you come to die, whether on the top of Pisgah or on the plains of Moab, you may fall asleep in Jesus, and have the bright and tranquil entrance into the blessedness of heaven.

VIII.—THE STONE ROLLED AWAY.

" Who shall roll us away the stone from the door of the sepulchre?"—This, communicants, was the earnest. inquiry of Mary Magdalene, and Mary, the mother of James and Salome, at a time when the brightest of their expectations seemed to be extinguished, and they were labouring under the pressure of the most overwhelming trial. Theirs, indeed, but a short time before had been the sad duty of standing around the cross of the blessed Redeemer, when all the other disciples had forsaken Him and fled, listening to the rude blasphemies of His mortal enemies, and gazing, with more than maternal anguish, on the dying agonies of Him whom their souls loved. And after the rest of one of the most solemn Sabbaths they had ever spent, they were now proceeding to the grave where the marred and broken body was reposing, for the purpose of embalming it with the fragrant spices they had brought with them.

It was a sad office which they were purposing to perform, and, assuredly, there was much to discourage and overwhelm them. For when they set out it was yet dark. The shades of night were falling heavily on their path. That

o

path was conducting them to the dread mansions of the dead. They themselves were unprotected and alone. Even the very body, which they sought with a feeling of the strongest affection, was guarded by the vigilance of their mortal enemies, while a great stone, which it seemed impossible for them to move, was rolled against the door of the sepulchre. And when we think of the difficulties that were thus rising up before them, we need not wonder that they were over-taken with the consciousness of their own help-lessness, and were disposed, with a feeling of despondency, to exclaim, "Who shall roll us away the stone from the door of the sepulchre?"

Yet wherefore these earnest inquiries, these appalling difficulties, these desponding appre-hensions? Were they justified by the circum-stances in which they were placed, or compatible with the exercise of a true faith in the promises which Christ Himself had given? No such thing. They had their existence only in the chambers of their own imaginations; they were the offspring of an unbelieving spirit; for when they came to the sepulchre and looked, the dark clouds were vanished, the stone was rolled away, the Saviour was risen.

Communicants, it is a possible thing that you may come to the table of communion with some-what of the same feelings that were prevailing

in the minds of these faithful but disconsolate
disciples. Yet wherefore should it be so, or why
should thoughts of despondency arise in your
hearts? The mightiest of all possible difficulties
is already removed. The stone is actually rolled
from the door of the sepulchre. The Saviour in
whom you trust has burst asunder the fetters of
death, and is seated at the right hand of the
Majesty on high, with the government of eternity on His shoulders, with the keys of death
and of hell in His right hand, bearing the name
before which every knee shall bow, and every
tongue confess that He is Lord to the glory of
God the Father. Go, then, if you will, to the
dark sepulchre, where He was once lying in the
depths of His humiliation, and there deposit the
weightiest of your burdens, and the black cata-
logue of your sins, and there let them lie buried,
along with the cast-off garments of the Saviour's
humiliation, in the grave of an everlasting forgetfulness, and let your lightened spirits make a
hasty escape from the gloom of the sepulchre to
the glory of the throne upon which He is now
seated, and see that you comport yourselves with
a spirit that is in harmony with the character of
that great Redeemer, before whom the poten-
tates and the immortalities of heaven are casting down their crowns, and who Himself is

wearing the titles and invested with the prerogatives of a king.

Communicants, is the stone removed? Is the sepulchre deserted? Is the Saviour risen? And will you still continue to seek the living among the dead? still hesitate to withdraw yourselves from the gloom that is associated with the sepulchre? still refuse to walk abroad amid the light, the consolations, and the glory that are shed around you by the morning of the resurrection? O fools, and slow of heart to believe, will you really tear the diadem from the head of the glorified Redeemer, and again open up the ghastly wounds of the crucifixion, and drag Him down from the splendours of heaven, that you may lay Him again amid the loathsomeness of the sepulchre? O fools, and slow of heart to believe, away with all your fragrant spices, your fancied merits, your fruitless lamentations, your clothing of sackcloth and ashes. The Saviour is risen and is glorified. The ensigns of royalty are all around Him. The whole treasures of heaven are placed at His disposal. And if you would rise along with Him and partake of His glories, you must be clothed in the likeness of the same image, and must seek the things that are above, where Christ sitteth at the right hand of God.

IX.—THE RISEN SAVIOUR.

" Then were the disciples glad when they saw the Lord."—And well they might, for they had previously been passing through a scene of doubt, and darkness, and perplexity, which had greatly staggered their faith, and almost extinguished their hope. First there was the mysterious agony through which the Saviour had passed in the garden of Gethsemane, when His sweat was like great drops of blood falling to the ground, while the prayer that broke from His troubled spirit was couched in these solemn and appalling words, " O my Father, if it be possible, let this cup pass from me ; nevertheless, not my will, but thine be done." Then there was the awful and the ignominious death to which He was subjected on the cross, when, amid the convulsions of nature, and the mockery and the blasphemies of a savage and infuriated mob, He bowed His head and gave up the ghost. And then, still further, there was the humiliation that was reserved for Him, when, in spite of all His stupendous miracles and the by-past revelations of His glory, He was removed out of their sight, and the great stone was rolled against the door of the sepulchre. These bitter and overwhelming trials, coming as they did in such rapid succession, were so contrary to all their previous expectations, that they seemed to have been plunged into the depths of an almost inconsolable distress, and had well-nigh come to the conclusion, that it was no longer He that was able to redeem Israel. Nevertheless, amid the pressure of these sore and overwhelming troubles, they did not forget the sanctity of the Sabbath, nor neglect the assembling of themselves together. It might be in a private dwelling, or an upper chamber, where they met, and, for fear of the Jews, the door might be shut where they were assembled together; but that was no bar to the entrance of the risen Redeemer. Silently, and in a moment suddenly, and without opening the closed doors, He stood in the midst of them, and shewed them His hands and His feet. And the result was instantaneous. In a moment all the dark clouds dissolved and disappeared. The sight of the great Redeemer,—the tortured, the crucified, the buried,—now risen from the dead, and living, and breathing, and speaking to them, and revealing the wounds of His lacerated body, came to them like life from the dead. The dark night of their sorrow and their weeping was changed into a morning of joy, the brightest they had ever yet been privileged to see. And having Christ with them as the fountain of all present consolations, and the hope of the everlasting glory, it seemed for the time being as if the days of their mourning were brought to a close. " Then were the disciples glad when they saw the Lord."

And so it is now, communicants. Christ is still to be seen. And if your eyes are opened, and you are anxious to see Him, there is no cloud, however dark, which His presence will not be able to dispel ; no burden, however weighty, which it will not be able to lighten ; and no grief, however poignant, which it will not be able to assuage.

It may be a dark and troubled spirit which you bring with you to the table ; but if you are looking earnestly unto Jesus, and laying all your burdens upon Him, He will prove unto you all that you need, and all that you desire. And if He stand in the midst of you, and breathe upon you with His life-giving Spirit, then for you, as there was to the disciples of old, there will be peace, true peace, the peace that passeth all understanding, the peace which this world can never give, and which, when given by Him, this world can never take away.

Oh, see that it be so with you. Let yours be something more than the prayer of the Psalmist, " Open thou mine eyes, that I may behold wondrous things out of thy law." Let yours be the petition, Open Thou mine eyes, that, like the inquiring Greeks, you may see Jesus, the chiefest of ten thousand, and altogether lovely. And in that case it will be well with you, well with you at the table, well with you in the family, well with you when you are journeying up through this wilderness, well with you when you pass through the dark valley of the shadow of death, well with you in the morning of the resurrection, well with you on the day of judgment, well with you when you pass through the gates into the city, and well with you for ever.

X.—THE CELESTIAL WORSHIPPERS.

" And I looked, and, lo, a Lamb stood on the mount Zion, and with him an hundred forty and four thousand, having his Father's name written in their foreheads. And I heard a voice from heaven, as the voice of many waters, and as the voice of a great thunder: and I heard the voice of harpers harping with their harps: and they sung as it were a new song before the throne, and before the four beasts, and the elders: and no man could learn that song but the hundred and forty and four thousand."

Communicants, whence came these hosts of celestial worshippers, these glorified associates of the Lamb that was slain? They are not beings that are removed to a vast and unapproachable distance away from you by the dignity of their rank, or the purity of their nature—beings between whom and yourselves there is established no bond of close communion. These are they which are redeemed from the earth. They were once the inhabitants of this fallen world. They possessed the character of miserable sinners like yourselves. They tabernacled for a season in dwellings like your own. They were liable to the influence of the very passions which you feel, exposed to the pressure of the very trials over which you mourn, tossed amid the swellings of the very Jordan which you dread ; and, peradventure, some of them were once the dwellers in your own neighbourhood, or the much loved and lamented members of your own families—the venerated parents, the warm-hearted sisters, the beloved brothers, the darling children that once abode beneath the covert of the same roof, and worshipped along with you within the walls of the same sanctuary, and sat with you side by side at the same communion table. And though you cannot now behold the radiance of their glorified faces, or listen to the accents of their heavenly voices, or

P

hear the mellifluous sounding of their celestial harps, nevertheless, you can draw comfort from the fact, that they are now ransomed from all their troubles, and are standing with the Lamb amid the glories of mount Zion, and are ascribing the wisdom and the glory, and the honour and the power, unto Him that sitteth upon the throne for ever and ever.

Blessed state! Is there a man amongst you that does not entertain the hope of realising it for himself? But what is the ground upon which your hope is resting? Here is the test: " These are they which follow the Lamb whithersoever he goeth." Followers of the Lamb—followers of His meekness, followers of His patience, followers of His mercy, followers of His gentleness, followers of His charity, followers of His purity, followers of His simplicity of character. Followers of the Lamb; but whither? Shall I say into the vanities and gaieties of a world that lieth in wickedness, or into the company and fellowship of men who make a mock at sin, or into scenes of mirth and revelry and pollution? Not there, surely, that the voice of the Lamb is to be heard—not there that the marks of His footsteps are to be traced. Follow Him into the closet, where secret prayer is wont to be made. Follow Him into the sanctuary, where He walketh amid the radiance of the golden candlesticks. Follow Him to the green pastures and the quiet waters, where He provides nourishment and refreshment for the wearied soul. Follow Him to the table of communion, where He sitteth down with His disciples, and maketh them glad with the joys of His salvation. Follow Him into the paths of righteousness, where He restores sweet comforts unto the soul, and leads you right onward to the gates of heaven.

Thus following the Lamb whithersoever He leadeth you, He will not only conduct you safely through all the paths of this earthly pilgrimage, but He will bring you at last to that bright and blessed land where you shall hunger no more, neither thirst any more, where the sun shall not light upon you, nor any heat, but where the Lamb which is in the midst of the throne shall feed you, and shall lead you unto living fountains of waters, and God shall wipe away all tears from your eyes.

XI.—GROUNDS FOR THANKSGIVING.

" Blessed be the God and Father of our Lord Jesus Christ, which according to his abundant

mercy hath begotten us again unto a lively
hope by the resurrection of Jesus Christ from
the dead, to an inheritance incorruptible, and
undefiled, and that fadeth not away, reserved in
heaven for you, who are kept by the power of
God through faith unto salvation ready to be
revealed in the last time."—This, communicants,
is a passage stored with unsearchable riches.
Every clause is replete with meaning. Not a
single word could be left out without bereaving
you of a treasure. All at once it arrests you
with the wealth which it spreads out before you,
and continues, from its commencement to its
close, to pour forth a flood of light, and of consolation, and of glory, which must leave you
utterly at a loss to comprehend what can be the
hope of your calling, and what the riches of the
glory of the inheritance in the saints, and what
the exceeding greatness of His power toward
you, and what the measure of that love of
Christ which passeth knowledge, and which
fills you with all the fulness of God. It is like
a Bible of itself; and if the truth it contains be
laid up in your hearts, and substantiated by
your faith, you can never be at a loss for subjects
of thought, and for sources of enjoyment, and
for themes of praise. You have all that the
most vigorous intellect can understand, and all
that the most necessitous spirit can need.

First of all, there is mercy, mercy for rebels ; mercy so abundant as to swallow up the vilest and the greatest of your sins. And besides mercy, there is hope, lively hope ; hope which neither the adversities of time nor the terrors of death can destroy ; hope which even now is like an anchor to the soul, both sure and stead-fast, entering into that within the vail. And not only hope, hope for the present ; but the object unto which hope looks—the object beyond the grave—the inheritance ;—the inheritance, how permanent! it is incorruptible;—how pure! it is undefiled;—how imperishable! it fadeth not away;—how secure! it is reserved in heaven, in the kingdom that can never be moved. And for the purpose of realising the mercy that pardons, and sustaining the hope that enlivens, and preparing for the inheritance that endures, there is also the power that keeps, the power that is irresistible—the power of God. And along with that power there is faith, precious faith, the faith whose end is the salvation of the soul. And the man who has an interest in the faith, and the hope, and the power of a salvation so pervaded by the mercy of God, so glorified by the resurrection of Christ, so inseparable from the inheritance of the saints, may well adopt the language of thanksgiving and praise, and exclaim, amid the experience of the hopes and consolations of the present, and in prospect of the glories and beatitudes of the future, "Blessed be the God and Father of our Lord Jesus Christ, which according to his abundant mercy hath begotten us again unto a lively hope by the resurrection of Jesus Christ from the dead, to an inheritance incorruptible, and undefiled, and that fadeth not away, reserved in heaven for you, who are kept by the power of God through faith unto salvation."

Communicants, do you profess to have an interest in the abundant mercy of God? then remember, that that is a mercy which has been purchased by the blood of Christ, and which can have no fellowship with sin. Therefore if it be yours, it will teach you to deny yourselves to all ungodliness and worldly affections, to live soberly, righteously, and godly in this present world.

Do you profess to have an interest in the lively hope which it is the province of the abundant mercy to produce? then remember, it is a hope unto which you have been begotten again, not of corruptible seed, but of incorruptible, even by the Word of God, which liveth and abideth for ever. Therefore it is a hope which must lead you to purify yourselves from all filthiness of the flesh and of the spirit; to purify yourselves even as Christ is pure.

Do you profess to have an interest in the inheritance that is reserved in heaven, the inheritance which has been brought to light by the resurrection of Christ from the dead? then remember, that it is not only an inheritance that is incorruptible, and which never fadeth away, but it is an inheritance that is undefiled. Nothing that is unclean can ever enter into it. It is an inheritance of saints. Therefore, beloved, seeing that ye look, according to His promise, for the new heavens and the new earth, wherein dwelleth righteousness, be ye diligent that ye may be found of Him in peace, without spot and blemish.

And, finally, do you profess to be kept by the power of God, the power that is able to save even to the uttermost? then remember, that that power unto salvation can be realised only through faith, the faith which worketh by love, the faith that overcometh the world, the faith that bringeth forth fruit to the praise and glory of God.

XII.—GOSPEL PRIVILEGES.

" Ye are come unto mount Zion, and unto the city of the living God, the heavenly Jerusalem, and to an innumerable company of angels, to the general assembly and church of the firstborn, which are written in heaven, and to God the Judge of all, and to the spirits of just men made perfect, and to Jesus the mediator of the new covenant, and to the blood of sprinkling, that speaketh better things than that of Abel."— These, believing communicants, are the privileges which you enjoy under the Gospel of the great Redeemer. Can you form a conception of a dispensation more glorious, more comprehensive, more ennobling, richer in its provisions, and more adapted to your own necessities? First of all, it finds you in the character of sinners, gazing in awful suspense on the blackness and darkness and tempests of Sinai, quailing amid the signs and the outbreakings of a wrath that is ready to devour; and having borne you hence, it leads you unto mount Zion, to the refuge which in Christ Jesus is opened up before you; and there you have a resting-place, defended by bulwarks that are stronger than the gates of hell, where the thunders and the tempests of Sinai cannot reach you, and all the darkness and the blackness disappear; for the glory of the Lord doth lighten it, and the Lamb is the light thereof. This is the first privilege. It brings you unto Zion, the city of the living God, the heavenly Jerusalem.

But it is not enough to have rescued the trembling criminal from the terrors of Sinai, and entrenched him in eternal safety within the broad and impregnable bulwarks of Zion. It leads him up from the strength of its foundations to the loftiness of its towers, and opens up vast prospects into the wide spaciousness of infinity, and comprehends within the boundlessness of its view the thrones and principalities of other worlds, the high ranks and orders of the loftiest intelligence ; and, drawing back the vail, it discloses myriads of angels looking into the great mystery of godliness, and ministering unto them who are the heirs of salvation. This is a second privilege. It brings you to an innumerable company of angels.

But there it stops not in the unfolding of its glories. It passes from the amplitude of space, peopled with these morning stars, these bright hosts of God, and it traverses the amplitude of time, congregating the elect ones into one vast and general assembly, drawing them out of all nations, and kindreds, and people, and tongues ; and, despite of all the distinctions of rank, and government, and age, enclosing them within the bonds of the same covenant, and leading them to the same home. This is a third privilege. It brings you to the general assembly and church of the firstborn, whose names are written in heaven.

Q

But not a half of its glory hath been told. It lifts you to an elevation that is higher still. It soars beyond the vastness of creation, and beyond the amplitude of space, and beyond the wide range of eternity. It crosses the awful gulf that lies between the finite and the infinite, and it leads you up to that nameless Being, whose essence no words of mortals can express—the supreme, the first, the last, the greatest, the wisest, and the best. Unto Him it brings you, to His very throne, and before that Judge of all it pronounces your acquittal, and sends you down with that acquittal to hold it up before the gates of hell, and in triumph to exclaim, " Who shall lay anything to the charge of God's elect? It is God himself that justifieth; who can condemn?" This is a fourth privilege. It brings you unto God the Judge of all, scattering all the terrors of the last day, and declaring the once guilty rebel righteous, and accepted in the beloved for ever.

It then comes to you as the children of affliction, walking, in the sorrowfulness of your souls, over all the silent and the solitary domain of death, suffering the pangs of bereavement, and weeping bitter tears over the dust of departed saints. It leads you away from that mouldering dust, though it tells you, for your comfort, that the dust itself is precious; that it is resting till the resurrection, and will be moulded anew into the form of immortal loveliness, and glorified. And it lifts your thoughts to the soul itself, and there it discloses it, not like the vile body, degenerating, undergoing the process of corruption, but clothed in glory, walking in uprightness, made perfect. This is a fifth privilege. It brings you to the spirits of the just, and unites you with a bond which neither death nor hell can ever break.

And, finally, and for the purpose of demonstrating the strength and immutability of the Gospel dispensation under which you live, it represents it as being placed in the hands of a Mediator—a Mediator in whom there is no feebleness, no partiality, no deceitfulness, no possibility of change, and no shadow of turning —a Mediator free from all the imperfections of sinners, and yet susceptible of all the sinless feelings of humanity, equal in power and dignity with God, and yet the very kinsman and surety of man. This is the final privilege. It brings you unto Jesus, the Mediator of the new covenant, and, cleansing you with His blood, it unites you unto Him, as He is united unto the Father; and being united, you can exclaim, in the language of an apostle, " Who shall separate from the love of Christ ? shall tribulation, or distress, or persecution, or famine, or nakedness, or peril,

or sword ? For I am persuaded, that neither
death, nor life, nor angels, nor principalities, nor
powers, nor things present, nor things to come,
nor height, nor depth, nor any other creature,
shall be able to separate us from the love of
God, which is in Christ Jesus our Lord."

Communicants, have you come unto mount
Zion, the city of the living God, the heavenly
Jerusalem ? Then live and act as the citizens
of Zion ; avail yourselves of the rights and immunities of the place ; bear about with you the
badges of your freedom ; and let the world see
that your conversation is in heaven,—" Walk
about Zion, and go round about her : tell the
towers thereof. Mark ye well her bulwarks, consider her palaces ; that ye may tell it to the
generation following. For this God is our God
for ever and ever : he will be our guide even
unto death."

Have you come to the innumerable company
of angels, those bright intelligences whose active
spirits are ever on the wing, who rest not day
and night, ministering to the heirs of salvation,
or singing before the throne, " Holy, holy, holy
is the Lord of hosts, the whole earth is full of
his glory" ? Then live and act as the comrades
of angels ; come out from the world and its
abominations ; seek to rise in nobleness of mind,
in purity of heart, in fervour of devotion, in ac-

tivity of zeal, to the hosts of God that are above
you, and shew, by the heavenliness of your
spirits, that there is something like a bond of
union between you.

Are you come to the general assembly and
church of the firstborn which are written in
heaven ?   Then live and act as the members of
that glorious assembly ; disgrace not your connection with the high and venerable church of
the firstborn ; bear upon your hearts the weight
of your responsibility ; and, remembering your
alliance with the spirits of the just made perfect,
let all malice, and envy, and evil speaking, be
banished for ever out of the midst of you, and
consider and provoke one another only unto love
and good works, for the interests of Zion, and for
the glory of Zion's King.

Are you come unto the Judge of all, and,
through faith in Him who is the Advocate with
the Father, have you come boldly unto His throne,
and been acquitted and justified by Him whose
decision no higher tribunal can ever question
or reverse ?   Then live and act as the justified
and the accepted of God ; stand fast, quit you
like men, be strong ; gird yourselves with the
whole armour of God ; and keep close to your
great Advocate, that He may defend you from
all evil, and be the joy and rejoicing of your
souls for ever.

And, finally, have you come unto Jesus, the Mediator of the new covenant, the daysman between God and your souls, and, united unto Him by faith and sprinkled with His blood, is He yours in all the riches of His grace, in all the plenitude of His power, in all the variety of His offices? Then see that ye forget not that you are His—His with all the members of your bodies, and all the faculties of your spirits, and all the weight of your influence; and being bought with a price, even with His precious blood, let it be your constant aim, in every place, and in all circumstances, to glorify Him in your bodies and your spirits, which are His. And " unto him that is able to keep you from falling, and to present you faultless before the presence of his glory with exceeding joy, to the only wise God our Saviour, be glory and majesty, dominion and power, both now and ever.   Amen."

DIRECTIONS AT THE CLOSE OF THE COMMUNION SERVICE.

I.—ISRAEL SET FORTH AS ENSAMPLES.

The children of Israel were the witnesses of the most signal miracles; they were the subjects of the most marvellous deliverances; they were admitted to the enjoyment of the most significant ordinances; but neither the cloud under which they walked, nor the sea through which they passed, nor the manna from heaven which they did eat, nor the water from the rock of Horeb which they did drink, was possessed of any virtue, either for the regeneration of their nature or the salvation of their souls. These were merely the outward and the visible signs of the spiritual and the heavenly grace; and because that grace was neither received into the heart, nor reduced to practice in the life, the mere outward rites had

no sanctifying influence and no saving power.
And what was the result? We are told that
with many of them God was not well pleased,
and, instead of being admitted into the rest of
the promised Canaan, they were overthrown in
the wilderness, or were destroyed of the destroyer.

These things, dear friends, happened unto
them for ensamples; and they are written for
your admonition, upon whom the ends of the
world are come, to the intent that ye should not
lust after evil things, as they also lusted. Neither
be ye idolaters, as were some of them. Neither
commit ye fornication, as some of them committed, and fell in one day three and twenty
thousand. Neither tempt ye Christ, as some of
them also tempted, and were destroyed of serpents. Neither murmur ye, as some of them also
murmured, and were destroyed of the destroyer.

But how can you avoid the course of backsliding and apostasy upon which the children of
Israel entered; and how can you escape the
punishment to which, in consequence, they were
subjected? For this end it is not enough that
you make a nominal profession of religion, or
engage occasionally in the most solemn ordinances of the Church of Christ, but your hearts
must be furnished with the grace of God; and
that grace, instead of lying dormant, or being

laid up in a napkin, like the talent of the unprofitable servant, must be laid out to good account,
and kept in a state of active operation. And in
what way ? Not, certainly, by investing you with
supernatural endowments, and divorcing you
from all fellowship with your brethren of mankind. That is what you have no right to reckon
upon. It is utterly at variance with the usual
mode of the Divine procedure. The grace of
God, if it be given to you at all, can never be
more profitably employed than in the faithful
discharge of ordinary duty, and the diligent improvement of ordinary means. If these are not
attended to, nothing else will make up for the
deficiency, and in that case it is impossible that
you can make progress in the path that leads to
heaven.

Now, this is a matter of great practical importance. You may desiderate something like the
working of miracles on the part of God, and you
may cherish some vague and indefinable expectation that He may send down upon you the
influences of His Holy Spirit in a moment suddenly, and in a manner altogether supernatural,
and in that case you may be utterly indifferent
as to the improvement of the outward and the
ordinary means that are placed within your
reach ; but in this you are compassing yourselves about with strong delusions, and enter-

R

taining hopes which are resting on no solid foundation, and which can never be realised.   If you
would make any progress at all, and have your
souls really prospering and in health before God,
and be brought at last to the end of your faith,
even to the salvation of your souls, you must not
only be looking with intensest earnestness for
the work of the Divine Spirit, but you must be
looking for it in the way of His own appoint-
ment, and in the use of ordinary means.   If
these be altogether neglected, or if they be but
partially attended to, there is no security whatever for the stability of your Christian charac-
ters, or for the salvation of your souls.   On the
contrary, there is every reason to expect that,
whatever be the profession which you make, or
however solemn the ordinances you observe, you
shall fall from your steadfastness, and go back,
to the perdition of your souls.   But if the smallest measure of Divine grace be yours, and you
diligently improve it in the ordinary way, giving
full proof of your fidelity, and making, day by
day, the utmost that you possibly can of the
Bible, the throne of grace, the Sabbath, the
sanctuary—then, in that case, it is impossible
that you can either go back, or that you can
stand still.   Your path, on the contrary, will be
like the light of the morning, which shineth
more and more unto the perfect day, and, instead

of becoming like evil men and seducers, worse and worse, you shall come nearer and nearer to the gates of heaven, and be made more and more meet to be partakers of the inheritance of the saints in light.

Such is the sum and substance of the directions which I tender to you after sitting down at the table of the Lord, and engaging in the sacred service. I do not ask you to leave the path upon which you are now walking, to give yourselves to the discharge of any peculiar or extraordinary duties, or to look for any communications on the part of the Divine Spirit which shall make you independent of the ordinary means of grace. I exhort you to search the Scriptures with all diligence, believing the doctrines which they teach, practising the duties they enjoin, and verifying the promises they record. I exhort you to make yourselves familiar with the mercy-seat, spreading out before it all your wants, making confession of all your sins, and asking, according to your circumstances, both for mercy to pardon and grace to help you in every time of need. And I exhort you, moreover, to give a regular attendance on all the services of the sanctuary, waiting upon God in His ordinances from week to week, and from Sabbath to Sabbath, with the earnest desire and the believing expectation that, through the promised blessing, they may be made life and spirit unto your souls. And, if you do so in faith and in godly sincerity, I do not doubt that, by these means, plain and ordinary as they may seem, you shall be conducted onwards in the path of Christian experience, till the process of your sanctification is complete, and an entrance is administered unto you abundantly into all the glories of the everlasting kingdom.

II.—THE PROMISE AND THE TOKEN.

" Certainly I will be with thee; and this shall be a token unto thee, that I have sent thee: when thou hast brought forth the people out of Egypt, ye shall serve God upon this mountain." —Such was the intimation which was given unto Moses when called by God to the great work of delivering the children of Israel out of Egypt, and when his own mind was much discouraged by the difficulties that were rising up before him. And it is an intimation specially deserving of notice, as one that is likely to be illustrated in the course of your personal experience. The first part of it contains a very comfortable promise—a promise of the presence of God; for God said, " Certainly I will be with thee." And

the second part adverts to a token by which
Moses was to know that the promise was fully
fulfilled, viz., that he was to serve God on the
mount of Horeb. What was the design of this?
Wherefore put the token at such an immeasurable distance from the promise? Why not associate them so closely together that the one
should follow immediately on the other? Would
not that have been more comfortable to the
mind of Moses, and prevented him from yielding
to a spirit of overwhelming despondency? Possibly it might. But would it have been more
beneficial? Where, then, had been his faith, or
the renown of the victory which his faith had
achieved? These had been awanting, and what
his soul may have gained in comfort he must
have lost in regard to the strength, and energy,
and stability of his Christian character. But
God adopts another and a wiser mode of procedure. He places the token, as it were, far
away from him, like some object concealed under
the verge of the horizon, and so distant as to be
invisible to the eye of sense ; and He appoints
him to travel through the whole intermediate
space—a space that was covered with difficulties,
and with dangers, and with trials, and, in the
meantime, or until he arrives at the substance of
the thing hoped for, all his support was the
simple promise, " Certainly I will be with thee."

Yet what else was it possible for a man of faith to need? What else was it consistent with the grace of God to give?

At all times, and in all circumstances, He is unto His people a kind and compassionate Father, dealing bountifully with them at the very time He is subjecting them to the chastisements of His hand, and withholding the tokens of His promises, or removing them to a great distance, for the purpose only of giving exercise to principles on which the blessedness of their souls depend. It is your part, therefore, simply to believe the promises on the testimony of God's own Word, and to give yourselves diligently to the use of the means with which they are connected; and, in the doing of that, you will assuredly be furnished with some token of the fulfilment of the promise. It may not be the clearest and the most decisive which it is possible for God to give; it may just be sufficient to encourage you onwards in the path on which you have entered, and to train you to the higher exercises of faith. As in the case of Moses, the clearest and most decisive of all tokens He may possibly reserve till the conflict is past, till the darkness of the night is gone, till the soul is ascended to the hill of God, and enshrined amid the light and the purity of heaven. There the tokens shall be decisive, the evidence of the fulfilment of the promises shall be complete; the assurance shall be perfect, the ways of God shall be all justified, and the darkest of His dispensations shall then appear as the best and the brightest.

———

III.—THE SHIFTING OF THE PILLAR OF FIRE.

When the children of Israel were about to pass through the perils of the Red Sea a remarkable change took place in the procedure of God. The command was given to them to go forward ; but the pillar of fire, the visible symbol of the Divine presence, instead of being placed directly in front of them, was removed from its position, and placed immediately behind. Thus all the scenery that was stretched out before them was marked with the mysterious and the indefinite, and, though God had not forsaken them, yet all their light came streaming in to them from the bright pillar that was behind. The darkness was all before them, but the glory of the Lord was their rereward.

So it may be with you, mourning disciple. The pillar that cheers and irradiates may have retired, as it were, to the rereward. All your

prospects may become dark, clouded, unpromis-
ing. Comfort to you at such a time may be a
word that has lost its meaning, or, if there be
ought like the semblance of it in the heart, it
may seem to flow in to you from behind, or to
come from those pillars of memorial which you
have raised, like Jacob, in the way through
which you have already passed, which, while
connected with the associations and remem-
brances of brighter and of happier days, constrain you, in the spirit of despondency, to exclaim, "O that I were as in months past, as in
the days when God preserved me, when his
candle shined upon my head, and when by his
light I walked through darkness, as I was in the
days of my youth, when the secret of God was
upon my tabernacle." Nevertheless, there is a
reason for the procedure of God, and if the light
of His countenance be partially withdrawn, and
the darkness of your prospects forces you to
revert with a melancholy pleasure only to the
days that are past, yet it may be that the same
cloud that is withdrawing the light from the
path that is before you, may be sending darkness
and destruction on the foes that are following
you from behind. At all events, the path of
duty is made plain. The command is given to
go forward. And though by so doing you may
seem to be leaving your consolations behind you,

and involving yourselves in conflict and perplexity—just as the children of Israel seemed to be hastening away from the light, and the protection, and the glory of the pillar of fire, while they were rushing forward to the sea of trouble, and of darkness, and of perplexity that was before them—yet, if you do go forward, the God of Israel will go forward with you, and the glory of the Lord will be your rereward. Your feet will be iron, and your shoes brass; yea, the eternal God Himself will be your refuge, and underneath you will be the everlasting arms. And His presence being with you, you will be conducted safely through all the trials of this earthly pilgrimage, and brought at last to that bright and blessed land where you shall hunger no more, neither thirst any more, where the sun shall not light upon you, nor any heat; for the Lamb which is in the midst of the throne shall feed you, and shall lead you unto living fountains of waters, and God shall wipe away all tears from your eyes.

IV.—THE UNSPEAKABLE GIFT.

Had God sent forth His ministering angels

8

to every corner of this vast universe, and summoned together the poorest and most miserable
of His creatures, and then sworn by Himself
that He would give to them the greatest gift
which any of their hearts could conceive, or
any of their tongues could ask, think you that
any frail child of mortality could have had
the boldness or the ambition to present himself before the throne, and, in the presence
of the Divine Majesty, to exclaim, " Lord God
Almighty, give unto us Thine own Son?" Impossible. Nothing within the range of an eternity could have lifted the mightiest spirit in the
universe to such a conception. It must have
lain for ever, even at the distance of infinity,
from the grasp or the approximation of anything that was created. Even the highest
archangel never could have soared so high, or
conceived how it was possible that such a gift
could be given—given to vile, self-condemned,
and hell-deserving sinners. And yet that is
the very gift which God hath given. He hath
not waited for your petition. He was prompted
to it by the movements of His own sovereign
compassion. And having given that greatest
of all gifts, there is nothing else which it is
possible for Him to withhold. The argument
of an apostle can never be gainsaid—" He
that spared not his own Son, but delivered him

up for us all, how shall he not with him also freely give us all things."

Dear friends, hath God given up His own Son for your sakes, and is there anything which you will refuse to sacrifice for His ?—any beloved lust, any ruling passion, any cherished idol, any worldly pleasure? If it be so, you have still much to learn in the school of Christ. You need to be brought more completely than ever under the influence of that most salutary admonition, " If any man will come after me, let him deny himself, and take up his cross and follow me." For " whosoever doth not bear his cross, and come after me, cannot be my disciple." A man looking to the cross of Christ, and professing to believe for himself that God did not spare His own Son, yet grudging in his inmost spirit to part with the vile portion of a carnal mind, calculating with a mean policy the utmost value of every earthly pleasure he is called upon to resign, and so incorporating himself with the pursuits and the spirit of the world as to be distinguished by little more than the parade of an empty profession,—that, surely, is not the temper and the complexion of a right-minded Christian.

Oh, believers, look to the cross of Christ, and lay hold of the fact that God did not spare His own Son, and shall there be any doubt about the consecration of every power, every talent, every possession, to His service? Oh, awake from your slumbers, and let your Christianity appear—not in mere outward profession: let it appear in the vigorous, well-sustained working which is the symptom of a healthy spirit. Look at the clouds of noble witnesses that are around you, and let your spirits rise from the dust, and hasten on. Hasten on, for the time is short, and the morning is past, and the shadows of the evening are closing in, and the night with its darkness is drawing nigh, and death is busy, and the throne of judgment is at hand, and the shadows of eternity are falling on the soul, and "all flesh is grass, and all the goodliness thereof is as the flower of the field; the grass withereth, the flower fadeth, because the Spirit of the Lord bloweth upon it; surely the people is grass." And watch ye, like holy watchers. For ye are weak, ye are helpless, ye are subject to vanity, ye are liable to temptation. And arise and pray. Pray with humble confidence. Pray with holy earnestness. Pray with spirits looking into eternity. Pray without ceasing. Watch every moment. Run with patience. Persevere unto the end. Be faithful unto death. The crown of glory is before you. The presence of God is with you. The blood of Christ is provided to cleanse you. The Holy

Spirit is promised to guide you. And may He who holdeth the crown, and who sprinkleth the blood, and who sendeth the Spirit, be with you, to strengthen you for the conflict, and at last to lift you into the everlasting glory.

V.—THE FAITH WHICH REMOVES MOUNTAINS.

It is well that you have faith to bring you to the table of communion, that you may feed upon Christ's fulness, even to the satisfying of your most enlarged desires. But your faith will lose the great recompense of reward, and the memory of it will pass away like a thing that is dead, if it do not go out into the world, and render itself immortal by palpable and imperishable deeds. All the saints of the olden time were men of faith, and their faith was of a high character, bringing them sensibly under the powers of an eternal world, carrying them up to the topmost glories of heaven, and changing them into the likeness of the Divine image, from glory to glory, as by the Spirit of the Lord. And their faith made itself apparent on the earth by heroic deeds, whereby, though now dead, they are still speaking. For though, in outward circumstances, they seemed of all men the most miserable, and in regard to privileges and opportunities of usefulness the most destitute, yet they wrought righteousness, they subdued kingdoms, they stopped the mouths of lions, they quenched the violence of fire, they turned the edge of the sword, out of weakness were made strong, waxed valiant in fight, turned to flight the armies of the aliens ; and by such means they not only obtained witness from God that they were righteous, but they also received upon the earth a good report, whereby their names and their noble deeds are held in everlasting remembrance.

It may be so in some respects with yourselves. At the same time, you must lay your account with occasional difficulties, and these difficulties may present a very formidable aspect. Like vast mountains, when contemplated by the unpractised eye, or when viewed from a great distance, they may seem altogether inaccessible, perfectly perpendicular, rising like a straight wall unto the very heavens, and, forming your judgment of them in such circumstances, you might be led at once to the conclusion, that to gain the summit of them, and to get over into the land that lies beyond, was nothing less than an impossibility. But if, instead of standing still, and judging according to the outward appearance, you are resolved to go forward with a bold heart, and with the determination, in God's strength, to surmount them, you will find, in the course of your personal experience, that there is nothing impracticable in the achievement. Your faith, though it were as small as a grain of mustard seed, will enable you to remove the mountains. And how? It may not arm you with supernatural power sufficient to lift them from their deep foundations, and to hurl them into the depths of the sea; but it will do what will answer the same end; it will invigorate your own minds with the energy, and the fortitude, and the endurance, and the perseverance, which will prompt you to go forward with the hope and the expectation of surmounting them. And what, in that case, will be the result? In the very act of advancing you will discover something like a change in the appearances of things. The very difficulties which seemed before to be insuperable, will appear to shift themselves to a greater distance the nearer you approach to them. When you begin actually to ascend, beaten paths will become visible, of whose existence you had no conception before. Pillars of memorial, erected by wayfaring men who have gone before you, will come prominently into view. And though there may be rugged places, where your feet are apt to stumble, and your hearts are ready to faint, yet there are also valleys where you can walk in perfect safety, green pastures where you can lie down amid your weariness, living waters bursting from the rock, with which you can refresh yourselves amid your faintings, and at every successive eminence views of such enchanting loveliness as will minister greatly to your enjoyment, and nerve you for the difficulties that are still before you. And thus, without the working of any miracle, but simply through the exercise of a patient and persevering spirit, you will mount up as if you had the wings of an eagle, and run without weariness, and walk without fainting. And when at last you reach the summit, and look down from your elevation upon all the way by which you have ascended, the toils and the perils will appear then as if they were nothing, the soul will be so transported with the magnificent prospects that are around you.

Therefore let me counsel you to remember, that the difficulties of the Christian life are not to be met by some supernatural agency that has no manner of connection with outward and ordinary means, nor are they to be subdued all at once, or by some mighty and stupendous efforts. The greatest of all results in regard to things temporal are brought about, for the most part, both by slow degrees and by a succession of isolated acts. And so it is also with regard to the interests of the soul. All things must not only be done in order, and according to established principles, but not unfrequently by little and little, one step preparing the way for another, and a succession of isolated acts terminating in fixed and enduring habits. Whether, therefore, you are just commencing your Christian course, or have attained to some goodly progress, there must be no standing still, no halting between two opinions, no slumbering, no sleeping. To the last hour of this mortal life there must be diligence and activity and perseverance. Even in death itself there must be no indecision, no shrinking back; and when you come to the dark and lonely valley into which it leads you, even then there must be a walking through, a going forward, till the darkness of mortality emerges into the brightness of heaven.

Keep, then, these principles in view. Improve, to the utmost of your power, every talent, however limited, which God has placed at your disposal. Be rigidly faithful in regard to matters which, of all others, may seem to be the most trifling. Be especially careful in the performance of ordinary duties. And instead of brooding over approaching difficulties, or standing aghast amid the trials that may be darkening around you, be it your part to go forward

T

with all your heart and strength and mind ; and
God Himself will be faithful in the fulfilment of
His own promise, " Fear thou not; for I am
with thee : be not dismayed ; for I am thy God:
I will strengthen thee ; yea, I will help thee ;
yea, I will uphold thee with the right hand of
my righteousness." "When thou passest through
the waters, I will be with thee ; and through
the rivers, they shall not overflow thee : when
thou walkest through the fire, thou shalt not be
burned ; neither shall the flame kindle upon
thee. For I am the Lord thy God, the Holy
One of Israel, thy Saviour."

VI.—THE DRAWING OF CHRIST, AND ITS RESULTS.

" Draw me, and we will run after thee."—There
is a peculiarity in the mode of expression made
use of in this prayer. It is not said, " Draw me,
and *I* will run after thee;" but the expression
is, " Draw *me*, and *we* will run after thee." The
drawing is a matter of personal experience.
Christ deals closely with each individual of His
people. Salvation is not thrust upon them
indiscriminately, nor are they saved in vast
crowds, merely because they wear certain exter-

nal badges, or give themselves to the observance of certain specified rites, or join themselves to the communion of some particular denomination;—"neither circumcision availeth anything, nor uncircumcision;"—but the man must become a new creature in Christ Jesus. For this purpose he must be emptied of all self-righteous claims, and brought into close and vital fellowship with Christ. And the drawing is of a character so personal, that the man feels as if the whole attractions of Christ's cross and the whole powers and prerogatives of Christ's Godhead were put forth, for the time being, on himself alone. Christ may be carrying on His work at the same time in the experience of hundreds, and thousands, and millions, and these may be placed in circumstances widely different from one another, yet the case of each individual is as carefully considered, and as fully provided for, as if there were no individual in the universe but himself. The prayer that passes from his lips is couched in these words, "Draw me." Yet the drawing in each case may not be precisely the same. The means adopted by the Divine Redeemer may be different. Some may be drawn by the attractions of the cross; others by the attractions of the crown. Some may be chosen in the furnace of affliction; others in the green pastures beside the quiet waters. Some of them may be drawn with a rod of iron, which subdues them by the power and severity of its inflictions; others may be drawn by the sceptre of peace, wielded by a hand which wipeth all tears from the mourner's eyes, and poureth into the bleeding soul the balm of a healing medicine. Yet the drawing comes closely home to the experience of each. He singles them out, as it were, one by one. He speaks to each as if he were standing isolated and alone. He knocks at the door of every heart, and these are His words, " I have redeemed thee ; I have called thee by thy name ; thou art mine."

But what is the legitimate result of this close dealing on the part of the Divine Redeemer ? Each individual soul is, in the first instance, drawn unto Christ Himself. That may be done secretly, silently, without observation. But the result is palpable and apparent. There is a running after Christ, a running after Him in the way of the Divine commandments, a' running after Him in close union with the other members of His family. The prayer for Christ's drawing may be offered up amid the secrecy of the closet. But when the prayer is heard, the man joins himself to the multitude of Christ's believing people, and in the face of open day, and in the presence of a great cloud of witnesses, he is seen running after Him. Thus there is a close con-

nection between the secret exercises of the heart
and the outward observances of the life, between
the secret drawing of the Divine Redeemer and
the open running of His people in the path of
His holy commandments. The things cannot
be separated. And wherever there is true faith,
the faith which unites the soul unto Christ, there
must be also the fellowship which joins you with
the family of the redeemed, and the running together, and in company, in the Christian race
which leads to the incorruptible crown.

VII.—CHRIST DWELLING IN THE HEART.

You have come, dear friends, to the table of
the Lord. You have publicly declared yourselves to be members of the Church of Christ.
You have eaten, in the presence of many witnesses, of the children's bread. And though it
may be that you are not yet filled with all the
fulness of God, yet, by joining in the communion
of saints, you have formally proclaimed that
Christ is dwelling in your hearts by faith. That,
at all events, is the profession which you have
made ; and it rests with yourselves to demon-
strate, by your conduct and conversation in the
world, whether it has been made by you in the

spirit of sincerity and truth.   If Christ is really dwelling in your hearts by faith, He will be there not only as the fountain of the sweetest consolations, and as the hope of everlasting glory, but He will be there also as the incentive to every heavenly affection, and as the spring of all holy and acceptable obedience.   The fulness that is in Christ will flow first of all into the believer's own heart, purifying his thoughts, his principles, and his imaginations, even at the very fountain, and carrying into every chamber of the inner man the odour of His sanctifying presence ; but, when it has filled the sanctuary of the heart, it will diffuse the same holy influence over all the issues of life, and bring the deportment of the outer man into beautiful conformity with the principles of a sanctified heart. And this we apprehend to be the meaning of that remarkable passage of Scripture when Christ stood and cried, saying, " If any man thirst, let him come unto me and drink.   He that believeth on me, as the scripture hath said, out of his belly shall flow rivers of living water."   In other words, the fulness of Christ was not only to flow into his own heart, to the ample satisfaction of his own desires, but Christ dwelling in the heart was to turn it, as it were, into a fountain whence rivers of living water were to flow forth for the comfort and the cleansing of vast multitudes around Him. Hence if Christ dwells in the heart of any man, it is not for the purpose of ministering merely to his personal gratification, and so filling him with the plenitude of His consolations as to shut him out from all association with a world that lieth in wickedness, or to render him altogether indifferent to every other interest but that which has reference to himself, but it is also to draw out the warm affections of the heart, and to turn him into an instrument of good to his brethren of mankind.

Therefore, keep these things in view, dear friends. Remember that yours is the character of social beings, who are connected by the strongest bonds with the whole family of the redeemed, whether they be in heaven or upon earth, and, therefore, it is befitting that you be so rooted and grounded in love, as to comprehend with all saints what is the breadth, and length, and depth, and height, of that love of Christ which passeth knowledge. But remember, moreover, that you are social beings, who are connected also by family ties, and by early associations, and by kindred sympathies, and by local attachments, and by business transactions, with other men who may not be belonging to the household of faith, but who, from the position in which they stand to you, and from the position in which you stand to them, are almost sure to be the recipients at

your hands, either of a large amount of good or
else of a large amount of evil. If you have been
with Jesus, and have made the solemn profession
that Christ is dwelling in your hearts by faith,
and if you shew by your tempers, or by your
conversation, or by the worldliness of your spirit,
or by the inconsistency of your conduct, that
your profession has been a matter of mere for-
mality, altogether unconnected with the principles
of vital godliness, and productive of no good
fruit, you may in that way be the instruments
of more real injury to the cause of Christ, and
to the spiritual well-being of those that are
around you, than if you had made an open and
undisguised profession of infidelity. But if you
carry your religious principles into all the familiar intercourse of everyday life, then it is not
for a moment to be doubted that whilst your
own souls will prosper all the more abundantly,
you will become the centre of an influence no
less powerful and beneficial upon all that are
connected with you.   Even without the putting
forth of any vigorous effort for the well-being of
other men, and by nothing more than the ex-
hibition of an humble and consistent walk with
God, you may become like the salt of the earth,
exercising a restraining influence on the atrocious wickedness of reprobate and ungodly men,
or, like lights of the world, so holding forth the

word of life in the face of a crooked and perverse generation, that others seeing your good works, and taking knowledge of you that you have been with Jesus, may be led to glorify your Father who is in heaven.

VIII.—PRIVILEGE AND TRIAL.

Were I to point to the communicant who, of all others, was most likely to experience the greatest revulsion of feeling, or who was in danger of suffering the most grievous fall, it would not be to the man who, during the services of a communion season, had been walking all the while in the lowest paths of the Valley of Humiliation, where everything around him, instead of basking in the bright sunshine, was covered, as it were, with clouds and with shadows. I should fix, rather, on the man whose buoyant spirit, emancipated from every restraint, had been mounting up as with the wings of an eagle, leaving all the clouds and the shadows beneath, and soaring upwards even to the very gates of heaven. The one may have been drawing water out of the wells of salvation, but without much sensible comfort, and with no remarkable enlargement of heart; and, without any extraordi-

u

nary effort, he may be enabled to go forward on the ordinary tenor of his way, and though there may be no rapid advances, no sudden elevation of spirit, which can stand comparison with the mounting up of an eagle, yet he may be passing over the ground with a pace which, though slow, is nevertheless so steady, that it may be truly said of him that he is running without weariness, that he is walking without fainting. But the other has risen to such an altitude above the level of his ordinary feelings, and been carried up so suddenly to the very top of the mount, and, all at once, has been so transported with the refulgent glories of the celestial world, that his spiritual vision, instead of becoming clearer than before, is apt to become dazzled with the excessive brightness; and not only so, but unless there be the continued outpouring upon him of Divine energy from on high, he must of necessity come down from the elevation to which he has risen, and, when the season of rapture and of excitement has passed by, the danger is that he may come down again, even from the very gates of heaven, as rapidly as he rose.

Therefore, let me remind you that seasons of special communion are likely to be followed with seasons of extraordinary trial, and that the sweetness of the consolations furnished by the one may be expected to be proportioned, in some degree, to the sifting and severity connected with the other. And hence it legitimately follows that seasons of extraordinary communion should be followed up on your part with seasons of extraordinary prayer, with the exercise of a spirit of extraordinary vigilance, and with the operation of a principle of extraordinary faith. This is the very thing you are in danger of neglecting, and, therefore, you are all the more likely to fall into the snares of the devil, and to be led captive by him at his will. Before engaging in the services of a communion season, there may have been, on your part, much anxiety of mind, and great searchings of heart, and the confession of many aggravated sins, and the pouring out of many earnest prayers for the presence of the Divine Redeemer, and for the consolations of His Holy Spirit. But if you have been greatly exercised before the Sabbath of communion came, you ought to be doubly so when the Sabbath of communion is past, for that is the very time in which there is the greatest danger of relapsing into spiritual indifference, and even falling into open sin. This we say to the young, and this we say to the old—to those who are girding on their armour at the commencement of their Christian course, and to those who are trimming their lamps for the coming of the Bridegroom. We say it unto one—we say it unto all.   And if any of you neglect the warning, of this you may rest assured, that in spite of all your comfort at the table, there is the strongest of all probabilities, that, falling from your steadfastness, you will impair the lustre of your Christian graces, and give great occasion to the enemies of the Lord to blaspheme.

IX.—NEED OF CLEANSING EVEN AT THE COMMUNION TABLE.

It was when the supper was ended, after the disciples had eaten of the bread which Christ had broken, and drank of the wine which Christ had poured out, that He girded Himself with a towel, and poured water into a basin, and applied Himself to the washing of their feet.   Even then, after all they had seen, and heard, and handled, and tasted, and done, there was a twofold process which they needed to undergo. They needed to be taught—to be taught the lesson of humility, and they needed to be cleansed— cleansed from the defilement of their sins.   The water that was poured into the basin for the washing of their feet, was not less necessary than the bread that was put upon the platter, or the wine which they had been drinking out of the cup. For there are sins, and shortcomings, and misconceptions appertaining to Christ's disciples, even when they are engaged with holy things. The communion of the sacred table is never altogether pure or unalloyed. Even in the most auspicious circumstances it is mingled with elements that are fitted to vex the Holy Spirit. It was while Judas was sitting at the table that the devil entered into his heart. No fences that were raised around it could keep him out. And he was busy, not only with Judas, the traitor and the apostate, but with all the rest. For, observe, it was not while they were walking through the fields, or conversing by the wayside, but it was while they were sitting at the table of communion, and after they had eaten of the broken bread, that the strife arose amongst them which led to the washing of their feet.

The origin of the quarrel was this: Jesus had just said to them, " Behold, the hand of him that betrayeth me is with me on the table." And then they began, not only to inquire among themselves " which of them it was that should do this thing," but there was also " a strife among them which of them should be accounted the greatest." I am not sure if I would be justified in saying, with perfect confidence, that Peter was the man that was taking the leading part in this unseemly strife; but there can be no doubt with regard to this point, that the devil was laying his snares for him no less than for Judas, for Christ singled him out from the rest, and said to him, " Simon, Simon, behold, Satan hath desired to have you, that he may sift you as wheat : but I have prayed for thee, that thy faith fail not." And then mark what was the counsel which He gave to him. Was it to seek the mastery over the other disciples ? No. It was to minister unto them—it was to help their infirmities. " When thou art converted, strengthen thy brethren." But in spite of this close dealing and this solemn warning, Peter was not convinced. He was still self-confident and presumptuous, loudly and impetuously pro-claiming, that whatever the others might do, as for him he was " ready to go both into prison, and to death." And we know what was the result. If he was really seeking for the highest place, he was doing it in a spirit which by a very rapid process hurled him down to the lowest.

Brethren, take warning. Be not highminded. Let the sad fall even of chosen apostles keep you cognisant of your own weakness. And after joining in the solemn service, and before leaving the sacred table, may the loving Redeemer not only sprinkle you with His precious blood, and wash you, that ye may be clean from all the guilt

that is past, but may He take you into His keeping, and pray for you, that, converted from every
false principle, and from every evil way, you
may shew yourselves not only to be living but
loving disciples, walking closely with the meek
and lowly Redeemer, and, like Him, seeking to
do nothing in the way of elevating yourselves,
seeking to do all in the way of glorifying the
Master and strengthening the brethren.

X.—THE STARLESS CROWN.

Dear Friends, if you have yourselves received
the grace of Christ, see that you make that grace
known. With the vows of Christ upon you,
cast your eyes around you, and you will find
some near neighbour, or some familiar acquaint-
ance, or some companion of your early years, or
some member, it may be, of your own household,
that is living without God, estranged from the
blessings of the great salvation, and dead in
trespasses and sins. Charge yourselves with the
responsibility of watching for such a soul. Make
the accomplishment of its salvation the burden
of your most earnest prayers before the mercy-
seat, and be as earnest in your endeavours for
its everlasting well-being as if you were the

keeper of that soul, and had to give an account of it at the bar of God. And praying, and labouring, and watching in faith, I do not doubt that, sooner or later, you will be able to set to your seal that God is true ; that, giving you the desire of your heart, you shall reap in due time if you faint not; that so, amid the radiant glories of heaven, you may have some one to stand associated with yourself as your crown of joy and rejoicing before the throne ; and that, looking around you on the souls for whom you have been watching, you may enter into the fulness of their joy, and rise yourselves to the glorious destiny—"They that be wise shall shine as the brightness of the firmament, and they that turn many to righteousness as the stars for ever and ever."

I heard lately of a young disciple. In her dying moments she had no doubt as to her personal interest in Christ. She had the comfortable assurance that she was just about to enter into " the rest that remaineth for the people of God." Yet a dark cloud passed over her countenance, and a heavy weight lay on her heart. What was the occasion of her grief? It was this. She had lived mainly to herself. She had not been the blessed instrument of leading one soul to Christ. She trusted that, through God's grace, she herself would be permitted to enter into the kingdom, but she feared that her's would be a starless crown.

A starless crown ! That I reckon to be the meanest crown in heaven, the crown that belongs to the lowest grades of the redeemed. The glory of the brightest crown in heaven consists not in its weight of finest gold. It consists in the number of its stars—in the lustre of its jewels. But where are these jewels to be gathered, and when ? Not on the golden pavements of heaven, when the watches of the dark night are past, but here, in this lower world, perhaps amid the dens of deepest and of darkest infamy —amid the filth and the offscourings of your very streets—amid the vilest sinks of pollution into which our poor humanity can fall.

Disciples of Christ ! The jewels are there. They are lying in thick masses around you, and they are as precious as the brightest gems in heaven. But their lustre is all dimmed. Gross darkness covers them. They are concealed and lost amid the filth and mire with which they are overlaid. But they are not lost irrecoverably. If you search for them as for hidden treasures, you may find them ; and by means of your strong faith, your heroic efforts, and your bowels of mercy, the lost may be found—the ruined outcast may be saved.

Let that noble work be yours. Live not unto

x

yourselves. Live evermore unto Christ, and for
Christ. If there be in the neighbourhood in
which you dwell one poor, ragged child, one
homeless orphan, for whose soul no one seems to
care, take you upon yourselves the burden and
the responsibility. If he be hungry, feed him.
If he be naked, clothe him. If he be sick, visit
him. If he be ignorant, instruct him. If he be
far away, and ready to perish, bring him to the
loving Saviour, and guide his wandering footsteps into the path that leads to heaven. And
verily you shall not lose your reward. What you
have done to the least of the little ones for
whom Christ died, will be reckoned as if it had
been done unto Himself. And the very jewel
which you have drawn from the mire, and lifted
from its low estate, will pass erelong to a higher
destiny ; and while plucked like a brand from
the burning, and set like a polished gem in the
Saviour's blood-bought diadem, it will add a star
to your own crown, which, like the great lights
of heaven, shall shine for ever, and for ever, and
for ever.

APPEAL

TO THOSE WHO ARE LIVING IN THE NEGLECT OF THE SAVIOUR'S DYING COMMAND.

IT is sad to think that there are individuals who are disposed to take credit to themselves because they have never joined in the solemn service of communion—individuals who, while chargeable with the guilt of neglecting the Saviour's dying command, are yet cherishing in their own hearts a certain feeling of complacency, because they are free, as they think, from the obligations which are lying on the professing disciples of Christ. Perhaps this volume may fall into the hands of some one who, yielding to the influence of such a feeling, has no fixed resolution, and no definite desire to take the vows of God upon himself by sitting down at the communion table.

Let me then, dear friend, appeal to your own

conscience, and let me ask you how the matter really stands with you? You just flatter yourself that you are more at liberty to live in sin than if you were to cast in your lot with Christ's disciples, and to sit down at the sacred table. Very well, take the comfort of that persuasion, but to what does it actually amount? Why, according to your own shewing, you are not, in point of fact, a servant of God at the present moment, nor in the meantime have you any desire to be so; and in that case you have no interest in His favour, no hold upon His promises, no title to the heaven which He has reserved for His people. And if you are not the servant of God, whose servant are you? Who is the master that is ruling over you? What are the wages for which you are working, and which you are well entitled to receive? You are the servant of your own corruptions; and are you not aware that the end of these things is misery, and bitterness, and death? You are the servant of the world; and are you satisfied with a portion so unsuited to the constitution of your nature—a portion which, in your very hands, is going down to dust and corruption? You are the servant of the devil; and have you laid your account with lying down with him for ever in the lake that burneth with fire and brimstone? That is your master; if you serve him faithfully, you need not be afraid that he will defraud you of your wages ; you may trust him to the full amount, and to the last farthing. But such wages for a rational and immortal spirit ! Are you content to receive them ? Will they bear you up amid the agonies of a hideous death, or amid the dread reckonings of a neglected judgment, or console you for ever for the loss of the beatitudes of heaven ? If they can, you are welcome to the comfort, and henceforth you may pride yourself in the thought that you have never joined in the service of communion.

But I dare not allow you to rest there. I warn you, that, after all, you are trusting in the grossest of all delusions. A man more at liberty to live in sin, because he is not a communicant ! Where is your warrant for such a doctrine ? What man is there within the borders of the universe who is at liberty, at any time, or in any circumstances, to continue in sin ? What man is there who can dare to continue in sin for a single hour without incurring the risk of eternal perdition ? And will you venture to purchase the liberty which may cost you such a fearful price ?

But I advance a step farther still. I proclaim to you that, though you have never seated yourself at the table of the Lord, the vows of God, nevertheless, are upon you. How is that ? You were baptized, were you not ? In that impressive ordinance you were devoted by your parents, and by your minister, to the service of God, and by virtue of it you are now a member of the visible Church of Christ. If, therefore, you have neither renounced your baptism, nor made an open profession of infidelity, there is actually lying upon your heart and conscience the responsibility of an engagement as binding as if you had seated yourself at the table of the Lord ; and if you still continue in your sins, of this you may rest assured, that the mere fact of your abstaining from the service of communion you will never be able to plead in arrest of the judgment you deserve. By reason of your baptismal engagement you must be dealt with and punished at the bar of God, not in the character of an ordinary sinner, but in the higher and more responsible character of a member of the visible Church of Christ ; and as a forewarning, which, I trust, will lead you to lay it to heart, I press upon you the solemn appeal of God Himself:— " A son honoureth his father, and a servant his master : if then I be a father, where is mine honour ? and if I be a master, where is my fear ? saith the Lord of hosts unto you that despise my name." And, " If ye will not hear, and if ye will not lay it to heart, to give glory unto my name, saith the Lord of hosts, I will even send a curse upon you, and I will curse your blessings : yea, I have cursed them already, because ye do not lay it to heart."

But I cannot leave you with the voice merely of warning, or with the prospect of impending judgment. I would rather seek to arrest you amid your waywardness, and to win you over by pointing you to the Saviour's bowels of mercy. The offers of the Gospel are still placed within your reach; the long-suffering Saviour is still waiting to be gracious; you have grieved Him; you have disobeyed Him; you have forgotten Him; you have dreaded Him; you have avoided Him; you have rebelled against Him; but He has not forgotten you, nor ceased to care for you, nor abandoned you utterly to yourself. He is a Father still, though His heart has been deeply wounded; and because He is a Father He hath sent forth to seek you; messenger after messenger has been despatched, some of them with rich gifts, some of them with solemn warnings, some of them with overtures of reconciliation; His word, His providence, His Spirit, His Sabbaths, His ordinances, His ministers, have every one of them been employed; yea, He Himself, with His tears, and His blood, and His dying agonies, has gone forth in quest of you, and even now He is calling upon you to arise and to return.

To resist such ineffable tenderness, to tamper with such long-suffering patience, to flee from the face of such a Saviour, is to trample upon your richest mercies, and with your own hand to affix the seal to your everlasting condemnation.

But to lay aside the enmity of the carnal heart, and, through the promptings of the Divine Spirit, to treat Him as a loving Father, to cast yourself at His feet, to rush into His outstretched arms, and to lay your head upon His bosom—that is the work of faith, the test of penitence, the way of acceptance, the earnest of forgiveness. And that forgiveness, dear reader, may be yours—yours now, yours freely, yours for ever. " Come now, and let us reason together, saith the Lord: though your sins be as scarlet, they shall be as white as snow ; though they be red like crimson, they shall be as wool." " Seek ye the Lord while he may be found, call ye upon him while he is near: let the wicked forsake his way, and the unrighteous man his thoughts: and let him return unto the Lord, and he will have mercy upon him; and to our God, for he will abundantly pardon." " Behold, now is the accepted time ; behold, now is the day of salvation."

C. GIBSON, PRINTER, THISTLE STREET, EDINBURGH.

LIST OF WORKS

PUBLISHED BY

JOHNSTONE, HUNTER, & CO.,

2 MELBOURNE PLACE.

EDINBURGH.

1865.

THE following are Wholesale Agents for Messrs JOHNSTONE, HUNTER, & Co.'s Publications; but copies of their Works may be obtained by order of any Bookseller in the kingdom.

LONDON.
HAMILTON, ADAMS, & CO.
SIMPKIN, MARSHALL, & CO.

MANCHESTER.
JOHN HEYWOOD.
W. BREMNER & CO.

LIVERPOOL.
WILLIAM GILLING.

BIRMINGHAM.
JAMES GUEST.

GLASGOW.
HUTCHESON CAMPBELL.

ABERDEEN.
LEWIS SMITH.
GEORGE DAVIDSON.

BELFAST.
C. AITCHISON.
A. S. MAYNE.
THE BIBLE AND COLPORTAGE SOCIETY FOR IRELAND AND ITS AGENTS.

MELBOURNE.
GEORGE ROBERTSON.

London Agents for the "Christian Treasury:"—
MESSRS GROOMBRIDGE & SONS, 5 PATERNOSTER ROW.

All Orders sent direct to the Publishers should be accompanied with a Remittance in Stamps, or by Post-office Order.

JOHNSTONE, HUNTER, & CO.'S LIST OF

HALF-CROWN VOLUMES.

NEW VOLUMES.—Just Ready.

I. THE CHILDREN OF THE GREAT KING. A STORY OF THE CRIMEAN WAR. By M. H., Author of " The Story of a Red Velvet Bible," etc. Extra foolscap 8vo, beautifully illustrated.

II. ATTITUDES AND ASPECTS OF THE DIVINE REDEEMER. By the Rev. J. A. WALLACE, Author of " Pastoral Recollections," etc. Extra fcap. 8vo.

III. PASTORAL RECOLLECTIONS. By the Rev. J. A. WALLACE, Hawick. Extra fcap. 8vo, cloth.

IV. OCEAN LAYS. Selected by the Rev. J. LONGMUIR, D.D., Free Mariners' Church, Aberdeen. Royal 16mo, cloth.

V. SUNDAY SCHOOL PHOTOGRAPHS. By the Rev. ALFRED TAYLOR, Bristol, Pennsylvania. With an Introduction by JOHN S. HART, LL.D., Philadelphia, U. S. Extra fcap. 8vo, cloth.

Lately Published.

VI. A PASTOR'S LEGACY; being Brief Extracts from the MSS. of the late Rev. R. B. NICHOL, Galashiels; with Introductory Notice by the Rev. J. A. WALLACE, Hawick. Extra fcap. 8vo, cloth.

VII. HISTORICAL NOTICES OF LADY YESTER'S CHURCH AND PARISH: Compiled from Authentic Sources. By JAMES J. HUNTER. Extra fcap. 8vo, cloth.

VIII. THE ANTIQUITY AND NATURE OF MAN. In Reply to the Recent Work of Sir Charles Lyell. By the Rev. JAMES BRODIE, A.M. Extra fcap. 8vo, cloth.

IX. LABOURERS IN THE VINEYARD; or, Dioramic Scenes in the Lives of Eminent Christians. By M. H. With Recommendatory Preface by the Rev. A. K. H. BOYD, Edinburgh. Extra fcap. 8vo, cloth.

X. A PRACTICAL VIEW OF CHRISTIANITY. By WILLIAM WILBERFORCE, Esq. New and Complete Edition. Royal 16mo, cloth.

XI. PRAYERS FOR THE CLOSET AND THE FAMILY. With Introductory Remarks on Prayer as a Christian Duty. By the Rev. GEORGE BURNS, D.D., Corstorphine. Royal 16mo, cloth.

XII. THE MYSTERY SOLVED: or, Ireland's Miseries: their Grand Cause and Cure. By the late Rev. EDWARD MARCUS DILL, A.M., M.D. Fcap. 8vo, cloth.

XIII. THE AFFLICTED'S REFUGE; or, Prayers adapted to Various Circumstances of Distress. Fcap. 8vo, cloth.

ILLUSTRATED GIFT BOOKS FOR YOUNG PEOPLE.

ELEGANTLY BOUND IN CLOTH,

PRICE ONE SHILLING EACH.

Nearly 30,000 copies have been sold of these elegant little Volumes.

Just Ready.

FRANK FIELDING; or, Debts and Difficulties.
A STORY FOR BOYS.

By AGNES VEITCH, Author of " Woodruffe," " The Fairy Ring," etc., etc.

Already Published.

I. THE STORY OF A RED VELVET BIBLE. By M. H., Author of "Labourers in the Vineyard," etc., etc.

II. ALICE LOWTHER; or, Grandmamma's Story about her Little Red Bible. By J. W. C., Author of "Mary M‘Neill," etc.

III. NOTHING TO DO; or, The Influence of a Life. By M. H., Author of " The Story of a Red Velvet Bible," etc.

IV. ALFRED AND THE LITTLE DOVE. By the Rev. F. A. KRUMMACHER, D.D.; and THE YOUNG SAVOY-ARD, by ERNEST HOLD. Translated from the German by a LADY.

V. MARY M‘NEILL; or, The Word Remembered. A Tale of Humble Life. By J. W. C., Author of " Alice Lowther," etc.

VI. HENRY MORGAN; or, The Sower and the Seed. By M. H., Author of " The Story of a Red Velvet Bible," etc.

VII. WITLESS WILLIE: The Idiot Boy. By the Author of " Mary Matheson," etc.

VIII. MARY MANSFIELD; or, No Time to be a Christian By M. H., Author of " The Story of a Red Velvet Bible." etc.

OTHER VOLUMES IN PREPARATION

WORKS BY JAMES BUCHANAN, D.D., LL.D.,

Professor of Systematic Theology, New College, Edinburgh.

In foolscap 8vo, Twenty-second Thousand, 2s. 6d.,

I. COMFORT IN AFFLICTION.

A few Copies for the Aged in Large Type, 8vo, 7s. 6d.

In foolscap 8vo, Eighth Thousand, price 2s. 6d.,

II. THE IMPROVEMENT OF AFFLICTION.

" We have not read any work on the subject which equals it, either in the substantial matter which it brings before the afflicted for their consolation, or in the variety of its details. Were we desirous, indeed, that affliction should be properly understood and improved, we could not recommend any book at all so well adapted for both purposes as this."—*The Scottish Guardian.*

In post 8vo, Seventh Thousand, 6s.,

III. THE OFFICE AND WORK OF THE HOLY SPIRIT.

" Every page shews the ripe divine, the eloquent writer, and the experienced Christian pastor. It is a felicitous mingling of argument and affectionate admonition."—*The Princeton Review.*

In foolscap 8vo, Second Edition, 1s. 6d.,

IV. ON THE " TRACTS FOR THE TIMES."

" Brief but comprehensive, clearly argued, and eloquently expressed. This is an admirable manual of Protestant truth."—*Watchman.*

In 2 vols. 8vo, 12s.,

V. FAITH IN GOD AND MODERN ATHEISM COMPARED.

" A work of which nothing less can be said, than that, both in spirit and substance, style and argument, it fixes irreversibly the name of its author as a leading classic in the Christian literature of Britain."—*News of the Churches.*

The following Chapters, each complete in itself, have been printed separately :—

DEVELOPMENT, 1s.; PANTHEISM, 1s.; MATERIALISM, 1s.; NATURAL LAWS, 1s.; SECULARISM, 1s.

In foolscap 8vo, price 3s. 6d.,

VI. THE " ESSAYS AND REVIEWS" EXAMINED.

" This is, perhaps, the most *complete* refutation of the Essayists which has yet appeared, and we cordially recommend it to the public."—*Clerical Journal.*

PROFESSOR BUCHANAN'S NEW WORK.

In One Volume, Demy 8vo, price 10s. 6d.,

ANALOGY

CONSIDERED AS A GUIDE TO TRUTH,
AND
APPLIED AS AN AID TO FAITH.

By the Rev. JAMES BUCHANAN, D.D., LL.D.,

Professor of Systematic Theology, New College, Edinburgh.

"This work is the fullest and most comprehensive discussion of Analogy as a guide to truth, and an aid to faith, with which we are acquainted, leaving untouched almost no question that has been raised respecting its true nature, its logical foundation, and its legitimate applications. We welcome the publication as a contribution equally interesting and valuable to the cause of science and religion, and one destined, we believe, to take a permanent place in the theological literature of England."—*Daily Review.*

"As a philosophical work, Dr Buchanan's 'Analogy' may justly claim a place beside the most meritorious dissertations on the intellectual powers; while the transcendent importance of analogical reasoning, as an aid to Christian faith, renders his elaborate and exhaustive treatise a welcome accession to scientific theology."—*Morning Post,* Jan. 1, 1864.

REPRINTS EDITED BY DR BUCHANAN.

WITH PREFACE AND NOTES.

I. PREJUDICES AGAINST THE GOSPEL.

By Rev. JOHN M'LAURIN, Glasgow, and JOHN INGLIS, D.D., Edinburgh. 1s. 6d.

"Masterly discussions on the foundations of the Christian faith."
—*The Weekly Review.*

II. THE USES OF CREEDS AND CONFESSIONS OF FAITH.

By PROFESSOR DUNLOP. 2s. 6d.

"Dunlop on 'The Uses of Creeds and Confessions,' is a work of high and permanent value, and the greater part of it is just as useful and seasonable now as when it was first published. We hope that many will embrace the present opportunity of becoming possessed of it."—*British and Foreign Evangelical Review.*

DR E. M. DILL'S WORKS ON POPERY.

Foolscap 8vo, price 2s. 6d., Sixth Thousand,

THE MYSTERY SOLVED;

Or, Ireland's Miseries: Their Grand Cause and Cure.

BY THE REV. EDWARD M. DILL, A.M., M.D.,

Late Secretary to the Scottish Reformation Society, and Missionary Agent of the Irish Presbyterian Church.

" A book fairly entitled to take its place among the best works upon the social condition of Ireland."—*Dublin University Magazine.*

By the same Author.

Fifth Thousand, foolscap 8vo, cloth, price 1s. 4d.,

THE GATHERING STORM;

OR, BRITAIN'S ROMEWARD CAREER:

A WARNING AND APPEAL TO BRITISH PROTESTANTS.

" Shall not the land tremble for this ? "—AMOS viii. 8.

" Righteousness exalteth a nation, but sin is a reproach to any people."—PROV. xiv. 34.

A very few Copies are now remaining of this able Work.

Foolscap 8vo, limp cloth, price 1s.,

PRELACY TRIED BY THE WORD OF GOD.

With an Appendix on the Prelatic Argument from Church History.

BY THE REV. JAMES N. MILLER, EDINBURGH.

" This little book might do some good service by being extensively circulated at the present time. It will offend no one, and is sure to give much knowledge as to the doctrine of Scripture on an important matter."—*Banner of Ulster.*

Third Edition, 18mo, cloth, price 1s.,

A MANUAL OF THE EVIDENCES OF CHRISTIANITY.

CHIEFLY INTENDED FOR YOUNG PERSONS.

BY JAMES STEELE,

Author of " The Philosophy of the Evidences of Christianity," &c.

NEW REWARD BOOKS.

In Ornamental Wrappers, price One Penny each,
With Beautiful Illustrations by CHARLES A. DOYLE,

SHORT TALES TO EXPLAIN HOMELY PROVERBS.

By M. H., Author of the "Red Velvet Bible," &c

No. 1. 'Who Gives Quickly Gives Twice.'
2. 'Short Accounts make Long Friends.'
3. 'Evil Communications Corrupt Good Manners.'
4. 'Forgive and Forget.'
5. 'Handsome is who Handsome does.'

No. 6. 'Better Late than Never.'
7. 'Do as You would be Done by.'
8. 'A Stitch in Time saves Nine.'
9. 'Where there's a Will there's a Way.'
10. 'All is not Gold that Glitters.'
11. 'Waste not, Want not.'
12. 'There is no Place like Home.'

The above, done up in a neat packet, price One Shilling.

Eighth Thousand, limp cloth, price 6d.,
WITH A RECOMMENDATORY PREFACE BY THE LATE REV. W. K. TWEEDIE, D.D.

THE SUFFERING SAVIOUR.

By THE LATE REV. JOHN MACDONALD, CALCUTTA.

Second Thousand, limp cloth, price 6d.,

THOUGHTS ON INTERCESSORY PRAYER.

By A LADY.

HABIT:

With special reference to the Formation of a Virtuous Character.
AN ADDRESS TO STUDENTS.

By BURNS THOMSON.

SECOND EDITION, REVISED. Price 2d.

WITH RECOMMENDATORY NOTE BY THE LATE PROF. MILLER.

Royal 32mo, price 8d.,

HYMNS FOR THE USE OF SABBATH SCHOOLS AND BIBLE CLASSES,

Selected by a Committee of Clergymen.

Second Edition, 18mo, sewed, price 4d.,

PRAYERS FOR THE USE OF SABBATH SCHOOLS.

By GEORGE BURNS, D.D.

*

CONFESSION OF FAITH.

(Italicised Edition.)　　Demy 12mo, cloth, price 1s. 6d.,

THE CONFESSION OF FAITH agreed upon at the Assembly of Divines at Westminster:

Together with the Larger and Shorter Catechisms, with the Scripture Proofs at Large; the Sum of Saving Knowledge, etc., etc.—In this Edition the *Italics* of the elegant Quarto Edition of 1658 are restored, by which those portions of the proof texts which bear *directly* on the doctrine advanced in each article of the "Confession" are clearly and precisely indicated.

Demy 12mo, cloth, price 1s. 6d.,

THE AUTHORISED STANDARDS

OF

THE FREE CHURCH OF SCOTLAND.

Comprising the CONFESSION OF FAITH, and other Authoritative Documents.

Published ┕ Authority of the General Assembly.

Second Edition, Crown 8vo, cloth, price 5s.,

REVISED TO 1862,

A DIGEST OF RULES AND PROCEDURE

IN THE INFERIOR COURTS OF

THE FREE CHURCH OF SCOTLAND.

WITH AN APPENDIX, EMBRACING A MINISTERIAL MANUAL, WITH FORMS AND DOCUMENTS.

BY THE LATE REV. ROBERT FORBES, A.M.,

Minister at Woodside, and Joint-Clerk of the F. C. Presbytery of Aberdeen.

In Extra Fcap. 8vo, printed on toned paper, price 2s. 6d., with Two Illustrations,

HISTORICAL NOTICES OF

LADY YESTER'S CHURCH AND PARISH, EDINBURGH.

Being the Substance of Four Lectures delivered before the Members of the Congregation. Compiled from Authentic Sources.

By JAS. J. HUNTER, Secretary to the Schools, &c.

STANDARD CATECHISMS.

I. THE ASSEMBLY'S SHORTER CATECHISM; with References to the Scripture Proofs. Demy 18mo, price 0½d., or 3s. 6d. per 100.

II. THE ASSEMBLY'S SHORTER CATECHISM; with (*Italicised*) Proofs from Scripture at full length; also with ADDITIONAL SCRIPTURE REFERENCES, selected from BOSTON, FISHER, M. HENRY, PATERSON, VINCENT, and others. Demy 18mo, price 1d., or 7s. per 100.

III. A CATECHISM OF THE EVIDENCES OF REVEALED RELIGION, with a few Preliminary Questions on Natural Religion. By WILLIAM FERRIE, D.D., Kilconquhar. Price 4d.

IV. A CATECHISM ON BAPTISM: in which are considered its Nature, its Subjects, and the Obligations resulting from it. By the late HENRY GREY, D.D., Edinburgh. Price 6d.

V. THE CHILD'S FIRST CATECHISM. Price 1d.

VI. A SHORT CATECHISM FOR YOUNG CHILDREN. By the Rev. JOHN BROWN, Haddington. Price 1d.

VII. A PLAIN CATECHISM FOR CHILDREN. By the Rev. MATTHEW HENRY. Price 1d.

VIII. FIFTY QUESTIONS CONCERNING THE LEADING DOCTRINES AND DUTIES OF THE GOSPEL; with Scripture Answers and parallel Texts. For the use of Sabbath Schools. Price 1d.

IX. A FORM OF EXAMINATION BEFORE THE COM-MUNION. Approved by the General Assembly of the Kirk of Scotland (1592), and appointed to be read in Families and Schools; with Proofs from Scripture (commonly known as "Craig's Catechism"). With a Recommendatory Note by the Rev. Dr CANDLISH, Rev. ALEXANDER MOODY STUART, and Rev. Dr HORATIUS BONAR. Price 1d.

X. THE MOTHER'S CATECHISM; being a Preparatory Help for the Young and Ignorant, to their easier under-standing The Assembly's Shorter Catechism. By the Rev. JOHN WILLISON, Dundee. Price 1d.

XI. WATTS' (DR ISAAC) JUVENILE HISTORICAL CATECHISMS OF THE OLD AND NEW TESTAMENTS; with numerous Scripture References, and a Selection of Hymns. Demy 18mo, price 1d.

WATTS' (DR ISAAC) DIVINE SONGS FOR CHILDREN;

With Scripture Proofs, for the use of Families and Schools. Price 3d.

SINGING AT SIGHT.

In neat Wrapper, Royal 8vo, price 1s., or cloth limp, price 1s. 6d.,

A GRADUATED COURSE

OF

ELEMENTARY INSTRUCTION IN SINGING

ON THE LETTER-NOTE METHOD.

(By means of which any difficulty of learning to sing from the common notation can be easily overcome.)

IN TWENTY-SIX LESSONS.

By DAVID COLVILLE AND GEORGE BENTLEY.

Also, in Two Parts, sold separately, price 3d. each,

"THE PUPIL'S HANDBOOK,"

Being the Exercises contained in the above Work, for the Use of Classes and Schools.

"Any advantage singers could gain from the study of the Sol-Fa notation, they appear to possess in this book, with the additional assistance which the staff imparts, as to the pitch of the sounds."—*Brighton Times.*

"We have very seldom indeed met with so good a manual."—*Aberdeen Journal.*

"We do not know a better or cheaper preceptor."—*Witness.*

"We think this publication is a step in the right direction, preferable to the systems of Curwen, Brechin, and others. . . . . The letter-note method retains the old notation in its entirety, and is applied from the very commencement to simplify it."—*Northern Warder.*

Nos. 1–8 now ready, price One Penny each,

THE JUNIOR COURSE

OF

ELEMENTARY INSTRUCTION IN SINGING

ON THE LETTER-NOTE METHOD.

By DAVID COLVILLE AND GEORGE BENTLEY.

FOR THE USE OF DAY OR SUNDAY SCHOOLS, JUNIOR CLASSES, ETC.

May also be used for Adult Male Voices by omitting the Bass.

CHEAP ELEMENTARY MUSIC.

Complete in Two Parts, price Fourpence each,

AN ELEMENTARY COURSE OF PRACTICE IN VOCAL MUSIC;

With numerous Tables, Diagrams, etc., and copious Examples of all
the usual Times, Keys, and Changes of Keys;

FOR USE IN CONNECTION WITH ANY METHOD OF SOLMIZATION.

By DAVID COLVILLE.

" We recommend all those engaged in teaching singing classes to
see this work."—*Northern Warder.*

CHEAP PART MUSIC.

CHORAL HARMONY,

IN VOCAL SCORE,

For the use of Choral Societies, Classes, Schools, etc.

Sections 1, 2, and 8, now ready, in stiffened Wrappers,
PRICE ONE SHILLING EACH.

LIST OF SEPARATE NUMBERS, PRICE ONE PENNY EACH.

*Those numbers marked † contain easy Music for Elementary or School practice.
Those marked * have an Accompaniment.*

SACRED.

3. O praise the Lord.		Colville.
6. Pray for the peace of Jerusalem.		
Hark, the loud triumphant strains. (12th Mass.)		Mozart.
†7. Brightest and best of the sons of the Morning. 3 v.		Webbe.
The Lord is my Shepherd.		Pleyel.
Be joyful in God.		Colville.
Characters used in Music.		
†8. Musical Signs and Abbreviations.		
How firm a foundation.		Mozart.
From Greenland's icy mountains.		Banister.
†11. To us a child of hope is born.		Mason.
Hark, the herald angels.		Arnold.
Hallelujah.		R. A. Smith.
14. Make a joyful noise.		R. A. Smith.
Sanctus.		Camidge.
15. Sing unto God.		R. A. Smith.

CHORAL HARMONY,—*Continued.*

17. Great God of Hosts ! · · · · · *Fowlie.*
    O God, forasmuch. · · · · · *Fowlie.*
*20. Blessed is he that considereth the poor. · · · *R. A. Smith.*
22. Hymn on Gratitude. · · · · *Holloway.*
*24. Come unto Me.
    Now to Him who can uphold us. · · · *R. A. Smith.*
26. O Father, whose almighty power   (*Judas*). · · *Handel.*
*28. There is a land of pure delight. · · · *Colville.*
*31 & 32. The earth is the Lord's. · · · *R. A. Smith.*
*35. Jerusalem, my glorious home. · · · *Mason.*
*38. Hear those soothing sounds ascending. · · *Beethoven.*
*39. Walk about Zion. · · · · *Bradbury.*
.   He shall come down like rain. · · · *Portogallo.*
*43. Blessed are those servants. · · · *J. J. S. Bird.*
    Enter not into judgment. · · , · *J. J. S. Bird.*
*47. Ode on resignation. · · · *Colville.*
†48. Hark, the Vesper Hymn. · · · *Russian.*
    The hour of prayer. · · · · *Douland.*
    Thanksgiving Anthem.
    God save the Queen.
†50. God bless our native land.
    Forgive, blest shade. · · · · *Callcott.*
    Morning Prayer. · · · · · *Herold.*
51. We come, in bright array   (*Judas*). · · *Handel.*
    Lead on, lead on   (*Judas*). · · · *Handel.*
†54. Ye gates, lift up your heads. · · · *Dr Thomson.*
    O send Thy light forth and Thy truth. · · *R. A. Smith.*
†56. Who is a patriot.
    Praise the Lord.
    Gently, Lord, O gently lead us. · · · *Spanish.*
    Joy to the world.
†59. With songs and honours. · · · · *Haydn.*
    Hymn of thanksgiving. · · · · *Mason.*
    God is near thee.
60. But in the last days. · · · · *Mason.*
*64. Great is the Lord. · · · · *American.*
    Arise, O Lord. · · · · · *American.*
*69. Awake, awake, put on thy strength, O Zion !
*70. I will bless the Lord at all times. · · · *R. A. Smith.*
*71. Hallelujah! The Lord God omnipotent reigneth. · *R. A. Smith.*
    God, the omnipotent ! · · · *Russian National Melody.*
†72. The brave man. · · · · · *H. G. Nogeli.*
    Lift up, O earth! · · · · · *G. F. Root.*
    From all that dwell below the skies.
    When shall we meet again.
    O wake, and let your songs resound. · · · *Himmel.*
    All hail the power of Jesus' name.
*75. Blessed be the Lord. · · · · *R. A. Smith.*
    Great and marvellous. · · · · *R. A. Smith.*
*77. Grant, we beseech Thee. · · · *Callcott.*
    Come unto Me when shadows darkly gather.
79. The Lord is my Shepherd. · · · *Beethoven.*
    Let Songs of endless praise. · · · *Mason.*
    My Faith looks up to Thee. · · · *Mason.*
81. Beyond the glittering starry sky. · · *J. Husband.*
82. Blest Jesus, gracious Saviour. · · *Michael Haydn.*
    Hymn of Eve. · · · · · *Dr Arne.*
    Salvation to our God.
84. I will arise. · · · · · *Richard Cecil.*
    Blessed are the people.
86. I was glad when they said unto me. · · · *Dr Callcott.*

SECULAR.

1. Let no dark'ning cloud annoy. - - - - -		*German.*
The Reapers. - - - - -		*Colville.*
2. There is a Ladye sweet and kind. - - -		*Ford.*
Gentle Spring. - - - - -		*Colville.*
4. And now we say to all, Good-night. - -		*Methfessel.*
The fountain. - - - - -		*Colville.*
5. Good Morning. - - - - -		*Bradbury.*
Swiftly, swiftly, glide we along. - - -		*Colville.*
†9. May-Day. *Colville.*—Harvest time. - -		*Storace.*
Glossary of musical terms.		
†10. Spring-time. *Silcher.*—Freedom. - -		*Scottish.*
Rosy May. *Scottish.*—The Daisies. - -		*Mozart.*
†12. Summer's Call. - - - - -		*Colville.*
Midnight. - - - - -		*Donizetti.*
13. Hark, the Curfew's solemn sound. 3 v. -		*Attwood.*
16. Serene and mild. - - - - -		*Webbe.*
18. How sweet, how fresh this vernal day. -		*Paxton.*
Stars of the summer night. - - -		*Cokking.*
19. Thyrsis, when he left me. - - - -		*Callcott.*
21. The Coquette. The Exquisite. - -		*Neithardt.*
Aldiborontiphoscophornio. 3 v. - -		*Callcott.*
23. Swiftly from the mountain's brow. - -		*Webbe.*
*25. It is better to laugh than be sighing. -		*Donizetti.*
27. Hark, the hollow wood surrounding. - -		*J. S. Smith.*
It was an English Ladye bright. - -		*Hine.*
†29. Joyful be. *Schneider.*—Sweet peace. -		*K. Smith.*
O lady fair. The last rose of summer. -		*Moore.*
30. The Skylark's song. - - - -		*Mendelssohn.*
Spring Morning. - - - -		*Schneider.*
†33. Come and join our trusty circle. - -		*Gabler.*
The Forest. *Karew.*—Sweet love loves May. -		*Silcher.*
*34. Glad May-day. - - - - -		*Neithardt.*
36. Good-night. - - - - -		*Hulme.*
Bright, bubbling fountain. - - -		*Waelrent.*
37. From Oberon, in fairyland. - - -		*Stevens.*
*38. The Chapel. - - - - -		*Kreutzer.*
†40. 'Tis dawn, the Lark is singing. - -		*G. Webb.*
Thrice hail, happy day. - - -		*German.*
Home! Home! - - - -		*Paz.*
Come joy, with merry roundelay. -		*German.*
41. Sweet Echo, sweetest nymph. - - -		*Birch.*
*42. The Gleaners. - - - - -		*Mendelssohn.*
*44. The Sight Singers. - - - -		*Martini.*
Hail, festal day. - - - -		*Rossini.*
45. Thy voice, O Harmony. - \ - -		*Webbe.*
46. Rural pleasure. - - - -		*Kreutzer.*
See the Sun's first gleam. - - -		*Schuffer.*
49. The Sprite Queen.		
The Sun's gay beam. - - - -		*Weber.*
Behold the morning gleaming. - - -		*Weber.*
52 & 53. All the Choruses usually performed in Locke's Music for Macbeth.		
55. Hall, smiling morn. - - - -		*Spofforth.*
See our oars with feather'd spray. - -		*Stevenson.*
57. Come, gentle Spring. - - - -		*Haydn.*
†58. Never forget the dear ones. 3 v. - -		*Root.*
Merrily o'er the waves we go. - -		*Bradbury.*
The Foot Traveller. - - - -		*Abt.*
61. The Chough and Crow. 3 v. - -		*Bishop.*
62. The huge globe has enough to do. 3 v. -		*Bishop.*
63. May Morning. - - - - -		*Flotow.*
Come to the woody dell. - - -		*Pelton.*
65. Which is the properest day to sing? - -		*Arne.*
Beat high, ye hearts. - - - -		*Kreutzer.*

CHORAL HARMONY,—*Continued.*

66. Now strike the strings.		Budd.
Since first I saw your face.	?	Ford.
67. Step together.		Irish Melody.
For Freedom, Honour, and Native Land.		Werner.
The Mountaineer.		Tyrolese Melody.
What delight, what joy rebounds.		German.
68. Come, let us all a Maying go.		L. Atterbury.
Hark, the Lark.		Dr Cooke.
Here in cool grot.		Lord Mornington.
*73. Come on the light winged gale. 3 or 4 v.		Callcott.
*74. Sleep, gentle Lady.		Bishop.
76. Sparkling little fountain.		Bradbury.
The dazzling air.		Evans.
*78. On Christmas Eve the bells were rung. 3 or 4 v.		P. King.
80. Hail, all hail, thou merry Month of May.		G. Shinn.
83. The sea, the sea, the open sea.		C. S. Neukomm.
85. The Singers.		C. Kreutzer.

The Series to be continued.

THE "AMPHION" GLEE AND ANTHEM BOOK.
EDITED BY DAVID COLVILLE.
In Penny Numbers.

SECULAR.

1. Upon the Poplar Bough.		Paxton.
4. Land of Light.		Kreutzer.
The richest land.		German.
6. The Song of the New Year.		Donizetti.
9. Lovely seems the Moon's fair lustre.		Callcott.
11. See the bright, the rosy Morning.		Blum.
12. How sweet the joy.		Kreutzer.
14. Forester sound the cheerful horn.		Bishop.
15 & 16. What shall he have that killed the deer.		Bishop.
My lady is as fair as fine.		Bennett.
20. Gaily launch and lightly row.		Mercadante.
22. Why should a sigh escape us? Parting Glee.		Otto.
23. Mountain home.		C. Kreutzer.
Over the summer sea. Arranged from the Barcarolle in		
Rigoletto.		Verdi.

SACRED.

2 & 3. Blessed is the people.		Righini.
Saviour, breathe an evening blessing.		Naumann.
5. Glory to God in the highest.		Heilwig.
Heavenly dwelling.		Nageli.
7 & 8. The God of Israel.		Rossini.
German Evening Hymn.		Lorens.
10. Sing to the Lord.		Haydn.
13. Hark, what mean those holy voices.		Naumann.
17. Evening Hymn at Sea.		R. A. Smith.
O Thou whose tender mercy.		Dowland.
18 & 19. I will cry unto God most high.		Zingarelli.
21. Sound the loud timbrel.		C. Avison.
24. Bless the Lord, O my soul.		Mozart.

This Publication is intended to supply Music of a less elementary character than that contained in "Choral Harmony." Each No. contains four pages of Music, with separate accompaniment.

Im TheStory

personalised classic books

"Beautiful gift.. lovely finish. My Niece loves it, so precious!"

Helen R Brumfieldon

★★★★★

JANE IN WONDERLAND

LEWIS CARROLL

UNIQUE GIFT

FOR KIDS, PARTNERS AND FRIENDS

Timeless books such as:

Kids

Alice in Wonderland • The Jungle Book • The Wonderful Wizard of Oz
Peter and Wendy • Robin Hood • The Prince and The Pauper
The Railway Children • Treasure Island • A Christmas Carol

Adults

Romeo and Juliet • Dracula

Highly Customizable   **Change** Books Title   **Replace** Character Names with yours   **Upload** Photo ffor inside page!   **Add** Inscriptions

Visit
Im TheStory.com
and order yours today!

WS - #0041 - 050822 - C0 - 229/152/12 - PB - 9780371933725 - Gloss Lamination